HEARTWOUNDS

The Impact of Unresolved Trauma and Grief on Relationships

TIAN DAYTON, PH.D.

Health Communications, Inc.
Deerfield Beach, Florida

www.hci-online.com

Library of Congress Cataloging-in-Publication Data

Dayton, Tian.
    Heartwounds: the impact of unresolved trauma and grief on
relationships / Tian Dayton.
        p.   cm.
    ISBN 1-55874-510-6 (pbk.)
    1. Grief. 2. Psychic trauma. 3. Loss (Psychology) 4. Interper-
sonal relations. 5. Interpersonal relations—Case studies. I. Title.
BF575.G7D396   1997   97-34760
158.2—dc21   CIP

©1997 Tian Dayton
ISBN 1-55874-510-6

Publisher: Health Communications, Inc.
                   3201 S.W. 15th Street
                   Deerfield Beach, Florida 33442-8190

Cover design by Tian Dayton, Ph.D.
Cover illustration by Aloys Wach

To Alex

Because you have
a heart that
understands.

There is a brokenness out of which comes the unbroken,
a shatteredness out of which blooms the unshatterable.

There is a sorrow beyond all grief which leads to joy
and a fragility out of whose depths emerges strength.

There is a hollow space too vast for words
through which we pass with each loss,
out of whose darkness we are sanctioned into being.

There is a cry deeper than all sound
whose serrated edges cut the heart as we break open
to the place inside which is unbreakable and whole,
   while learning to sing.

Rashani
Cofounder of Earthsong,
a woman's sanctuary in Hawaii

• CONTENTS •

III. The Effect of Trauma on Relationships.........85

IV. Transformation and Healing Through Grief..131

V. The Personal Journey 191

Charts

✦ ACKNOWLEDGMENTS ✦

This is a book of personal stories and research woven together to illustrate and analyze the impact that unresolved trauma and grief can have on relationships throughout life. It could not have been written by research alone. It is the people whose stories are witnessed on these pages who have breathed life and given form and shape to the role that unresolved trauma and grief issues can play in undermining otherwise healthy relationships. I appreciate them, not only for their willingness and honesty but because we have undertaken a portion of each other's destiny. We have been partners in our mutual soulmaking. It is a central tenet of psychodrama that in a therapy group, each person becomes a therapeutic agent in each other's healing process. I would like to acknowledge these healers who have played such an important part in each other's growth.

I would like to thank my Monday night group, clients, psychodrama trainees and students at New York University for sharing their stories with me and with the reader. Their lives are the inspiration for the contents of this book. I feel privileged to have been a part of their journeys and fortunate to be allowed to reveal them in these pages. It is my hope that you, the reader, will see a piece of your own life reflected back to you in this communal sharing of the deepest side of human nature that they have allowed me to bring forward. In the interest of anonymity, all names have been changed.

There are others to whom I am indebted who have helped move this material from literally piles of research into a work that will hopefully be beneficial and comprehensible. Roy Carlisle, through his editorial wisdom, his years of experience in publishing, and his spiritual depth, has helped to yank, cajole, pull and encourage this book out of me and I am ever grateful. Christine Belleris is, as always, helpful, insightful, professional and generous in her demanding role at Health Communications. Gary Seidler and Peter Vegso took this idea seriously and felt it was an important enough subject to support even though, in marketplace terms, it is risky to talk about a subject of such weight. In today's publishing climate of blockbuster books and "tell alls," I really appreciate their wish to help people in meaningful ways. Phoebe Atkinson has handed me pieces of research that caught her penetrating eye and enhanced these pages. And Toby Bielawski helped at a crucial point to give a shape that could hold this material and make it accessible.

I also gratefully acknowledge the brilliant research on the subject of grief and trauma of such professionals as Bessel van der Kolk, M.D., Judith Herman, M.D., John Bowlby, M.D., George H. Pollock, M.D., Ph.D., Ester R. Shapiro, Ph.D., and Therese Rando, Ph.D.

As this book goes to press three lives of archetypal significance have passed from this world leaving in their wake an unprecedented outpouring of both grief at their passing and gratitude for their contributions. In acknowledgment of Diana, princess of Wales, Mother Teresa and Victor Frankel who gave us permission to open our hearts to the pain of life and transform its energy into purposeful action while carrying a message of love and hope to the world.

✦ INTRODUCTION ✦

*Take this sorrow onto thy heart, and make
it a part of thee, and it shall nourish
thee till thou art strong again.*

LONGFELLOW, HYPERION

T he use of intimate relationships as a path toward deepening a relationship with self and God is one of the highest callings of intimacy. I have come full circle. As a baby boomer I came of age in the late 1960s and early 1970s. Until then the word "unconscious" had little meaning—it seemed as if it belonged to a realm beyond the reach of human understanding. The idea that each of us had one, and that it had stored within it great pieces of who we were, felt almost hocus-pocus. But we searched. We searched everything from Freud to *Autobiography of a Yogi*. What was this unseen, amorphous thing that had so much power over our daily decisions and our life thrust? More mysterious still was the thought of such a phenomenon as a collective unconscious. For years I studied Eastern thought, attempting to gain an understanding of something like a deeper self. Until then the world, I thought, was as it appeared, and people were simply who they thought or said they were. As a cultural group we turned our known world upside down in an attempt to get a better look at it, but it appears to me now that in doing so we simply got a different look at it.

I learned to befriend my unconscious in college. Books I read and courses I studied suggested to me that there was a part of me that lay hidden in my inner depths that I could invite to play a positive role in my life. Practicing positive thinking, opening to abundance, trading negative self-concepts for positive ones were all ways that I could use this storehouse of untapped personal power to flow in a direction that I encouraged. My thinking could act as a rudder, steering the vessel of me through the waters of my life in a direction that I could, in some measure, self-determine. It wasn't until later in my life when I entered my own recovery process that I also came to understand that my unconscious was a vast storehouse in which I had slowly accumulated the records of my own life history. The idea that what was stored in this unconscious had tremendous power over my thinking, feeling and behavior, over decisions as wide-ranging as what I chose for lunch to whom I chose to marry, took longer for me to fully grasp.

My first real encounter with this, I suppose, was in marriage. I knew I would marry my husband from the first, but if I told you (or myself) why, it would make little sense; though to a deeper part of me, it felt as inevitable as the rising or setting of the sun. If I say it was his glance, or the way he held me when we danced or how I felt when we went grocery shopping together, it would seem superficial; and yet, 23 years later, I understand that it was my unconscious talking to me, reaching out from its shadowy depths to touch itself, to insure the continuance of the very experiences that I had held so dear in my relationships with my own father and mother. He felt as familiar as my own insides, though

I hardly really knew him. I understand this today as a sort of re-remembering, reacquainting myself with experiences matching those stored in my memory bank, long forgotten—imprinted onto my brain in childhood. It has always been easy to keep the child in me alive in my relationship with my husband because the child in me chose him for better or for worse. I was drawn toward what I had known and forgotten. The child in me was saying yes, this is familiar—this is what you know. The lucky thing for me is that even though my family was deeply wounded by addiction and divorce, my father and mother loved me. So when I again looked for deep intimacy, I reached not only for what was famil-iar in all ways, some healthy and some not—I reached also for love because, on an experiential level, I knew what love *felt* like. I was unconsciously looking to replace the love and comfort I had experienced as a small child and lost, to repair a painful past, to have security and family in my life again.

I remember the vows my husband and I took 23 years ago when we invited both God and other people into our relation-ship. At the time we were deeply involved in studying yoga and Eastern philosophy. We had traveled to India together in search of a spiritual life. Like so many of our generation, we wanted to understand what life was really about. Like so many baby boomers, we grew up with countless material advantages and learned the disillusioning lesson that possessions and position, though they were indeed good fortune, did not necessarily ensure inner peace or success in love relationships.

Each of us had divorced parents and each of us carried deep wounds as well as riches in the area of intimacy. We had an over-powering desire to restore what we had loved and lost. My par-ents divorced when I was 14, and my father died when I was 23, but throughout the years after his divorce he would take me aside and tell me that he would always love my mother, that she was a good woman, that their divorce hurt me and that he was sorry for that. When she remarried, he called her husband to tell him he was marrying a fine woman and to wish them happiness. It seems to me that in his old-world way, he was trying to correct the past and do what he could to allow life to go on for those he loved—even if he could not participate.

My father came to this country at 16, having run away from a seminary education in Greece to seek his fortune in America. He was not fluent in the English language and had $16 in his pocket. Though a truly brilliant man, he didn't have the advantages that he gave me—no therapy or higher education—but he knew the path of the human spirit, and he did what he could to remove the knife from our hearts. In his old Greek wisdom he understood modeling that if I felt he did not love my mother, I would feel I could not be loved by a man in that forever kind of way. By telling me he would always love her, he told me that I could be loved, too. The sheer size and expression of his love has been a source of strength that I have drawn upon throughout my life.

My husband and I made promises to each other as we walked around the altar. Some I don't even remember, but the one that has always stayed with me was the last: "You will be my friend in life—here's to a lifelong friendship, friend." That commitment has helped us to give and dig deeply, even at times when we thought we had nothing left to give each other. We could take a break and come back and try again. When we couldn't find a solution to a problem, we prayed for one. At one point in our marriage ceremony we faced each other and repeated the same words simultaneously. "When you are distant, I am close; when I am distant, you are close." I have always been so grateful for those words because they told me we could take turns, that we wouldn't always be in the same place at the same time, that one of us could lead the other through the dark and scary corridors of intimacy. If one of us could stay on track, then we could bring the other one along until we could plateau again. This gave both of us the strength to do the difficult inner work we needed in order to use our relationship to heal old wounds. When my abandonment fears got so triggered that I would rather bolt from the relationship than feel, his wisdom could pull me back; and when his engulfment fears grew so intense that he wanted to escape the relationship that was triggering them, my steadiness could weather it for both of us. The gifts that we have given each other in this way have allowed us both to become the people we wished to be and have the life we wished to have.

Our emotional and psychological blocks that kept us afraid of getting close were carried within each of us—the relationship triggered them, but they were not only about the relationship. In any case, until we worked out unresolved issues, we were not able to identify present from past pain. Once we could clear out the unresolved pain from yesterday, the old baggage and trans-ference reactions, we could react to each other in the present. This made conflicts immeasurably easier to solve because hurt feelings were just hurt feelings about what happened today, and not weighed down by decades of repressed hurt from the past that had been triggered by a present-day circumstance.

Much of this work is also the work of the spirit. Cleansing the "lower self," as yogis would say, or purifying the "nous" or "intel-lect," as in the Eastern Orthodox tradition, is part of the path toward God consciousness. The blocks that we carry that keep us from being fully intimate in a relationship are often the blocks that keep us from being fully intimate with God and life. They are the dead wood of the repressed unconscious—numbness, unre-solved anger, despair and yearning. When the unconscious is asked to contain all of this in unacknowledged silence, there is little breathing space to allow for the lightness and serenity that are part of higher consciousness. However, despair and yearning are a path toward God if they are channeled in that direction by surrendering to and exploring the contents of the feeling, rather than denying or repressing it. Compassion is born out of just this sort of search; before we can gain the ability to feel for another person, we need to be able to feel for ourselves, to sit with our own woundedness and brokenness until it becomes spiritual. The transformative power of intimacy provides the vehicle to get in touch with both the wound and the love. I had to miss my father before I could risk fully loving my husband, and the love we feel for each other is the community that we share with our children and our world. It expands the container of self, the door through which higher consciousness enters.

Drop a pebble in the water and it will create a series of ripples that resonate far beyond its seemingly innocuous entrance into the lake. Then it will sink to the bottom of the lake, where it will join the vast array of pebbles that make up the water's floor. So it is with life experiences. Each experience, happy or sad, upbuilding or demeaning, has a ripple effect in the mind and then sinks or is stored in the lake of the unconscious. This storehouse of the unconscious becomes a script imprinted in the vast and subtle network of the brain, out from which we draw our information for living—from which we learn the lines that get acted out on the stage of our lives. How we behave in relationships is informed by what lies in the storehouse of our unconscious mind and gets recalled with split-second accuracy when our relationship acts as an experiential trigger of unresolved pain and hurt.

In Part I of this book we define trauma and map out the stages of grief and mourning we pass through in order to heal. We will also list the warning signs of unresolved grief and trauma.

In Part II we outline the personality changes that can occur as a result of trauma; those issues that resonate and shape personality development and impact our thinking, feeling and behavior.

In Part III we explore and discuss the effects that those personality changes have on our ability to sustain healthy relationships in our lives. We will trace how and where unresolved pain from the past surfaces and gets played out or reenacted in present-day relationships; and how we can choose to use that pain either to get stuck in a cycle of creating more pain or to show us where we need to grow.

In Part IV we explore the relationship between grief and spiritual growth. We see how grief can open the heart to receive grace and wisdom.

In Part V we have our Personal Journal. This is a series of user-friendly exercises that allow the reader to explore personal issues that may be affecting his or her relationships.

The grey pages after sections I, II, and III describe the basic underlying concepts that are the root of grief and trauma.

The circular charts at the beginning of each section outline the impact of trauma on the personality which assists the reader in developing a mental picture or map of the overall process of transforming wounds into wisdom.

Parts II and *III* of this book are particularly challenging. Some of the material may require a bit of extra effort to comprehend and it may also bring up feelings as you read it. With any luck you will see aspects of your own life flash across your mind as you read. I have tried to make the material as accessible as possible and to use case studies to illustrate points. Though the reading in these sections is dense at times, I feel that once you get through it, you will be able to wrap your mind around a complicated and fascinating subject because, after all, what is more interesting to us than the mechanics and mysteries of our own inner world?

Part IV discusses the rewards and the beauty that can come into life as an outgrowth of plowing through pain and *Part V* is your section; it is for you, the reader, to use in any way that you wish.

It is my wish that this book will combine the excellent theory available on grief and trauma in a way that will fascinate and challenge you as much as it did me to research and write it. I hope that you will both enjoy this book and find it helpful in creating a more fulfilling life and healthier, happier relationships.

I wish you well.

PART I

Loss and Trauma

Aloys Wach

1

The Resonance of Traum

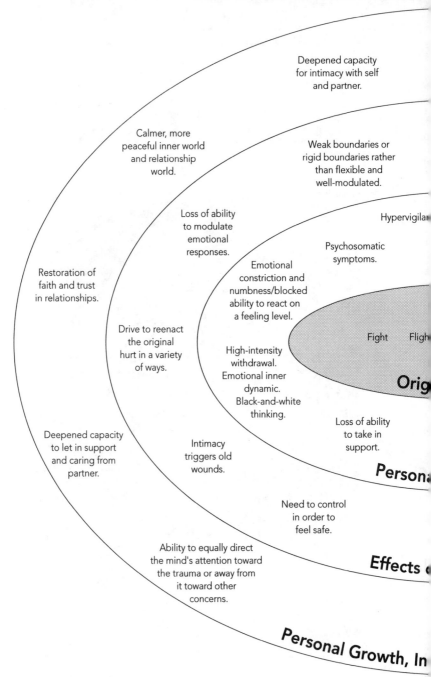

Deepened capacity
for intimacy with self
and partner.

Calmer, more
peaceful inner world
and relationship
world.

Weak boundaries or
rigid boundaries rather
than flexible and
well-modulated.

Loss of ability
to modulate
emotional
responses.

Hypervigila

Psychosomatic
symptoms.

Emotional
constriction and
numbness/blocked
ability to react on
a feeling level.

Restoration of
faith and trust
in relationships.

Drive to reenact
the original
hurt in a variety
of ways.

High-intensity
withdrawal.
Emotional inner
dynamic.
Black-and-white
thinking.

Fight   Fligh

Orig

Loss of ability
to take in
support.

Deepened capacity
to let in support
and caring from
partner.

Intimacy
triggers old
wounds.

Person

Need to control
in order to
feel safe.

Ability to equally direct
the mind's attention toward
the trauma or away from
it toward other
concerns.

Effects

Personal Growth, In

om Hurt to Healing

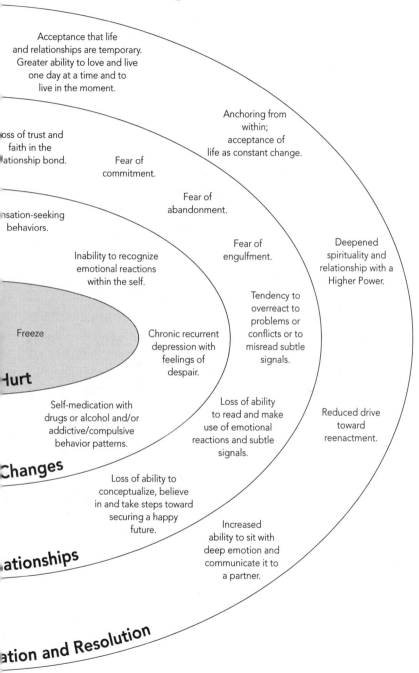

Acceptance that life and relationships are temporary. Greater ability to love and live one day at a time and to live in the moment.

Anchoring from within; acceptance of life as constant change.

oss of trust and faith in the lationship bond.

Fear of commitment.

Fear of abandonment.

nsation-seeking behaviors.

Inability to recognize emotional reactions within the self.

Fear of engulfment.

Deepened spirituality and relationship with a Higher Power.

Freeze

Chronic recurrent depression with feelings of despair.

Tendency to overreact to problems or conflicts or to misread subtle signals.

Hurt

Self-medication with drugs or alcohol and/or addictive/compulsive behavior patterns.

Loss of ability to read and make use of emotional reactions and subtle signals.

Reduced drive toward reenactment.

Changes

Loss of ability to conceptualize, believe in and take steps toward securing a happy future.

Increased ability to sit with deep emotion and communicate it to a partner.

ationships

ation and Resolution

twounds

Happiness is beneficial for the body, but it is grief that develops the powers of the mind.

Marcel Proust, *Remembrance of Things Past: The Past Recaptured*

There is far too much talk of love and grief benumbing the faculties, turning the hair gray, and destroying a man's interest in his work.
Grief has made many a man look younger.

William McFee, "On a Balcony," *Harbours of Memory*

Great grief is a divine and terrible radiance which transfigures the wretched.

Victor Hugo, "Fantine," *Les Miserables*

Sorrow is one of the vibrations that prove the fact of living.

Antoine de Saint-Exupéry, *Wind, Sand and Stars*

There is no grief so great as that for a dead heart.

Chinese proverb

Loss and Trauma

The tragedy is not that a man dies,
the tragedy of life is what dies
inside a man while he lives.

ALBERT SCHWEITZER

The Wound That Can't Be Seen:
Healing the Wounded Heart

A ny creature that bonds grieves when it experiences separation—whether it be an elephant kicked out of the herd, a duck that has lost its mate or a mother who sends her child off to college. As humans, we are biologically designed to form kinship bonds through which we learn the lessons of love, caring and intimacy. When those bonds are broken, a piece of us breaks or is traumatized by that loss. Then we go through life hungry for what is missing. When we avoid the experience of grief, we lock ourselves up in the loss; we carry around an unhealed wound.

Humans are physical beings, existing in time and space. Scientists tell us today that our *emotional bodies* are just as physical as our corporeal bodies—only harder to see and measure. Healing is biologically driven: We cut ourselves, we clean and suture the wound. Then we rely on nature to complete our healing process. We cannot reknit our flesh, but nature can. So it is with emotional wounds. Wounds to the heart need to be cleaned in order to naturally heal. A wound to the psychospiritual body can be just as crippling to the whole person as a wound to the physical body.

Life is full of losses. Passing wholly through the stages of mourning—whether it be for a loved one, a job, a divorce, a child who has left home or a stage of life—not only strengthens the ego and the inner self, but increases our trust in life's ability to repair and renew itself. It deepens our inner relationship with the self.

Grieving serves a number of important functions. It releases the pain surrounding an event or situation so that it will not be held within the emotional and physical self. Grieving allows the wound to heal. If we do not grieve, we build walls around the ungrieved wound in order to protect it, even though these very walls can keep healing experiences out as well.

I have asked myself a thousand times what is the difference between a person who can live a healthy balanced life and one who cannot seem to get life together in a productive manner. We all face problems. But some people move through them and some remain stuck. I have observed that clients who succeed in therapy exhibit or acquire certain qualities:

They are able to *self-reflect*—that is, they look at their own thinking, feeling and behavior and have enough emotional distance from their self-identification so that they see themselves realistically.

They *take their own good advice and live by it* rather than spending valuable time and energy digging trenches, then sitting in and defending them.

They *identify what they are feeling* and *articulate it to themselves and others,* which gives them the ability to face the pain of loss.

They *identify their issues* and live with a realistic rather than an idealized view of themselves, and when life hurts they are able to *own* their issues and work *with* them.

They cope with loss by *calling it by its correct name,* and *move through* the *emotional turmoil* of a grieving process.

They *separate the past from the present,* which allows them to live in today without sabotaging it with unresolved, unfinished business from the past.

They *find meaning and purpose* in their struggle, which is how spiritual transformation and growth take place.

They use life struggles not only to *get through* but to *grow,* thus deepening and strengthening their relationship with life and self and others.

I find it very exciting and hopeful to see this process at work. Over and over again I have seen lives that were in shambles turn around and become happy and productive. I have witnessed people who were caught in chronic despair awaken to their own pain, process it and get better. These are not overnight miracles. They are not the result of thinking the right thought, going to the cutting-edge seminar or seeing the perfect therapist. They are the result of surrendering to the grief process, having the courage and willingness to walk through it and the commitment to stay with it for *as long as it takes.* Healing is a series of quiet awakenings, born of the willingness to struggle to have a true and honest encounter with the self.

We have, in attempting to explain the complexities of the human mind and our relationship with self, created the field of psychology. But in our quest to contain and describe pathology, we have forgotten the philosophical roots of the field. The philosophers of ancient times took on no less of a goal than to better understand the whole of the human spirit, body, mind and soul. The ancient Greeks and yogis did not research representative control groups, but spent their lives in lifelong contemplation and observation, first of self and then of others. They looked at humans and attempted to order the functions of both mind and spirit. When psychology ignores the spirit, it goes its way without a conscience, without that very energy that first gave it life. Without a spiritual philosophy, life is reduced to only what we see. Scientific observation has expanded too much for life to be reduced to this narrow and superficial vision.

The field of psychology expanded very quickly after World War II in order to address the traumas of war, and perhaps this partially explains why its focus has remained so pathologically oriented. Perhaps this happened because psychology made its alliance with the Newtonian model of science, and broke off from philosophy and art. But the human spirit has always sought to express itself at the deepest level through art, writing, music and ritual. These are the voices of the soul, the vehicles through which inner turmoil and grief are worked through and brought from silence into song, through shadow into light. Throughout time we have expressed our humanness through the vehicles of body, mind, heart and soul. Possibly a society less inhibited in this personal expression would have less need for violence and less buried hurt flowing into the underground river of emotional isolation and psychological illness.

We can suffer loss in many ways. A person can be lost not only to death but to divorce, addiction, separation or alienation. The stages of *mourning* and *bereavement* following the death of a loved one are similar to what I observe people go through in the process of therapy, whether or not they have lost a loved one to death. Often the people I see in the field of addictions have lost a loved one to addiction, divorce or mental illness. In the case of children of divorce, the children lose the warmth and reliability of both parents in the home. They often feel left behind and deeply confused. "If Daddy can't get along with Mommy, then how can I? Should I move away too? What happened to our family?" Similarly, the children of alcoholics may still have the parent in the home, but they have lost access to their loved one. Their loved one is there, but emotionally the experience of those children is that their mother or father is lost to them, a prisoner of their addiction and unavailable to the children who need them. Often children of parents with psychiatric disorders such as clinical depression or psychosis feel that they can neither emotionally or psychologically *find* their parents, nor can they rely on them to help them with their own developmental needs on a consistent basis. Children who are physically, emotionally or sexually abused may feel the loss of innocence or childhood.

Clients that I serve seem to need to go through a process of active grieving of early childhood losses in order to be able to move into adult roles. If they do not go through this, and if they remain locked in the pain associated with early loss, they unconsciously have such a strong yearning for the original lost object (person or experience) that they spend much of their time hoping, wishing and trying to make their present-day adult situations into relationships and careers that will give them what they lost—which is, of course, not possible. Consequently, they move through cycles of excitement and disappointment, disillusionment and abandonment of their endeavor that closely mirror their earlier experience and serve to retraumatize them. Their access to adult roles is blocked because they are stuck in the unfinished business associated with their child roles. These are wounds that can go unattended in our need to "get on with life." Oftentimes, these ungrieved wounds lead to emotional problems and depression later in life.

Where do the grief and sadness and fear go when we, as a society, no longer honor the depth of loss and support someone through it? We seem to see feelings of grief as a sign of weakness rather than strength. In fact, true grieving both requires a strong ego and builds a strong ego because it asks us to stand beside our own pain and allow ourselves to have it. It asks us to be strong and compassionate and wise enough to hold our own woundedness in our hearts without abandoning ourselves at this very crucial moment. There is nothing weak about this. It is a sign of love and contact with what is real and alive in this world, and it requires the wisdom to give ourselves the right to be human.

The aforementioned are dramatic types of losses, but as we live our lives, we experience various ranges of loss on many levels. The loss of youth, the loss of our physical strength and prowess as we get older, the loss of hair, the loss of beauty, the loss of career, the empty nest syndrome—the list goes on. How we learn to cope with loss greatly influences how deeply we allow ourselves to experience life, and how successfully we are able to modify old roles and adopt new ones.

Giving Voice to the Wound

There are two concepts of catharsis: the Aristotelian one of purging inner pain, and the one that arises out of Eastern religion that holds that "a saint, in order to become a savior, [has] first to save himself" (Moreno, 1946). In other words, he has to become self-actualized. "Catharsis" in Greek means to cleanse. Working with and through pain is one of the ways that cleansing occurs within a person. Whether the pain is self-imposed, as in the case of the aesthetic, or visited upon us by a life circumstance out of our control, it can burn away the attachments and preoccupations of the ego-centered self. Orthodox psychotherapy, too, sees self-purification as the first task of the therapist or priest before and while helping others: "Physician, heal thyself" (Luke: 4:23). According to Andrite Vlachos, a Greek Orthodox theologian, "The truly physician-like nous (mind, intellect) is the one that first heals itself and then heals others of the diseases of which it has been cured" (*Orthodox Psychotherapy*, 1994). We might say that one aspect of grief is totally self-centered while another is universal, illuminating our deepest and most intense attachments in life. Then, in a spiritual awakening, we surrender control and the belief that anything is everlasting except the soul, the seed of life itself.

Filling an Empty Hole

Hurt people search the world for just the right relationship that will make everything all right forever, that will fill the empty hole, provide missed nurturing and give them the life, love and security that got derailed because of trauma. They become fixated on finding it and so begin a lifelong search, but they search for the wrong thing and they search in the wrong places. Their black-and-white thinking causes them to see the solution to their problem as being *a* solution, *a* person, *a* job and so on. Each new relationship becomes a hope for being saved, for turning their life around. When the person disappoints or the job is less than wished for, they return to a position of helplessness, seeing themselves once again as having been cheated. Rather than look within themselves to find out what they are doing (or not doing) to contribute to the emptiness they feel, they look outside. "I've made another bad decision," "I only choose unavailable, messed-up people," "My boss is impossible" and so on. Their very hurt and irrational shame render them unable to turn the microscope back upon

themselves to ask the hard questions that would lead to a resolution rather than a repetition.

When people or animals are traumatized, they rely on primitive survival strategies. *Fight, flight* and *freeze* are survival mechanisms. They allow us to get through a situation alive, but they
do nothing to help us resolve or integrate. They flood the brain
and body with chemicals that put the system on red alert and
are designed to help us cope with danger or acute stress. When
they are burdened through overuse, they can affect a person's
ability to assess normal situations. Later in life, victims of trauma
assess each situation as if it were a threat or a danger, and the
intensity that these trauma survivors carry within themselves
distorts their reaction to normal life circumstances, inhibiting
their ability to have normal relationships. They see danger
where it doesn't exist, offense where none was intended. They
attach themselves anxiously to people, driving them away
because of their neediness. The fact that they have not learned
to modulate their interactions with people means that they tend
to overreact, shut down or withdraw (fight, freeze and flight).
So once again they fall back onto their black-and-white thinking, which in this case manifests as "I made the wrong choice
again," "Things will be fine when I find the right person—this
was the wrong one" and so on. Because of this kind of all-or-
nothing thinking, they are unable to stand back, assess a relationship and make appropriate adjustments to make it work. To
fit themselves into the relationship and the relationship into
themselves; to compromise, adjust and work it out. Instead,
their life comes to mirror their trauma reaction—intense
involvement or withdrawal, nothing in between.

Often, trauma survivors don't understand what compromise
feels like; they experience it as a loss of self because they haven't
learned how to stay connected with another person or situation
while maintaining a sense of self—to modulate their inner world

and, by extension, their outer world. They repeat rather than resolve, react rather than listen, and withdraw or fuse rather than engage. Or they may go on automatic pilot, remaining physically in the relationship while on the inside they have broken their connection with it. They interact with their intellect, doing what they think is called for, but they shut off the part of themselves that interprets on a feeling level, and their interaction is based not on what they feel and sense but on what they think. They lose their ability to pick up and interpret the subtle cues that would help them read the relationship dynamics and adjust themselves, or else they overreact to signals, reading into them more than is there. The all-or-nothing relational pattern is a direct result of shutting down the nonsurvival systems such as emotions.

Compounding this, trauma survivors frequently use liquor and drugs to medicate the pain and isolation that they experience, reaching for a chemical solution to their problems. This is why, when addicts get sober, they are often in emotional pain. After their "medication" is removed, they are once again confronted with the unresolved pain that drove them to drink in the first place. If we resolve traumas, we cry the tears and feel the fear and abandonment that we could not afford to feel at the time of immediate danger. If we don't resolve those traumas, we shut down our inner world and function in the outer world just as we did then, with the same defenses we used at the time of the original hurt.

This pattern explains in part why trauma survivors so often re-create high-stress relationships: They are drawn to that level of external intensity, as it matches up with the intensity of their inner world. They are, in a sense, wired for intensity and have trouble living with nuance, which requires modulating their emotional responses and making subtle adjustments to adapt to the natural vicissitudes of a relationship. Trauma is an interruption of the attachment bond, and it alters our ability to attach in healthy, well-modulated ways, whether that relationship be with the self or another person. The ability to relate becomes impaired. The sad truth is that no person or situation can fully heal a survivor of cumulative trauma or piled-up hurts until such time as that person also engages in healing from within. The outside relationship can provide the person with a vehicle through which to heal, to relearn how to relate, but until the survivor is able to learn, meaningful change will probably not take place. Trauma survivors need relationships and groups in which to reawaken the self that went under for protection. They need to be vulnerable, to feel their feelings rather than shut them down—but until they are able to stop projecting their pain by blaming others for it, they will not be able to reflect upon themselves enough to heal, to take responsibility and ownership for what goes on inside of them, to get honest first with themselves and then with others. People who have accumulated negative effects from loss or trauma need to pass through active stages of grief and mourning in order to get on with their lives in healthy, rather than unhealthy, ways.

Divorce: The Hidden Wound

We are at a cultural crossroads that changes the way we apply our understanding of grief and trauma issues. Nowhere is this more evident than in the changing institution of marriage. In the life of a husband and wife, "till death us do part" was the norm until the 1950s. In this century alone we have added two-and-a-half decades to the average life span of each individual. In other words, "till death us do part" is 25 years longer than in previous centuries. This may be one of the reasons why we have seen the divorce rate skyrocket, approaching 50 percent of the married population. The prospect of spending two or three decades in one marriage has led to a reassessment of the commitment. While divorce itself has become commonplace, its pain and the sense of loss that it engenders are far-reaching and profound. Religious institutions have had rituals in place for centuries that deal very effectively with loss through death, but none that deal with the grief attendant upon loss through divorce, because divorce was not the same issue when life itself was shorter and families were a central economic and procreative institution.

Divorce is actually a more complicated loss than death when it comes to issues of mourning because it robs both spouses and children of their family continuity and dramatically reorganizes family relationships. When divorce is not openly mourned by spouses, children and all of the other extended family members that it affects, the grief goes underground. Where does it go? The answer to this is staring us right in the face, though it is often missed and mislabeled:

- It gets played out in the crowded court system in the form of protracted legal battles that are vehicles for unresolved pain and anger.
- It gets dramatized in painful and complicated custody battles that turn children into unsuspecting carriers of family grief.
- It gets acted out by children through aberrant behavior and drops in performance at school.
- It carries over into subsequent, often premature, relationships that become burdened with unresolved pain from previous relationships.
- It leaks into the family system where it is mistaken for present pain. Natural dissention within the family is made more potent by unresolved past anger making normal family problems feel overwhelming.
- It erupts on the streets and spills into the penal system through young people who have inadequate support systems to meet their developmental needs.

- It leads to drug and alcohol addiction, the outcome of misguided attempts to numb the emotional pain that follows the trauma of loss.

Society still does not know what to do with divorce. And yet it is our collective inability to deal with the pain that allows it to spill over into virtually any or all areas of our individual lives and relationships.

We will work with these and other wounds caused by separation, loss and addiction as well as problems in dealing with other losses such as job loss, relocation and normal maturational life losses.

How I Got Here

Initially I was attracted to this subject, I thought, because I consistently saw clients with unresolved grief and trauma issues. After years of training on how to identify particular problems, interpret thoughts, feelings and behaviors, I eventually came to feel that each and every person I saw who carried unhealed wounds within, hungered to be nurtured and accepted. What these people really needed from me as a therapist, as much as clever interpretation or specific goals, was a place to come with their tears. The interpretation and goals were important, but they came later.

Next, grief and trauma theory provided a way out—through a process called mourning. Most people traumatized by life losses or acute stress need to pass through an active process of mourning so they can heal.

Often it is just this process that is denied them, simply because so many acute stresses and losses come from living in dysfunctional families, and dysfunctional or highly stressed families tend to hide and deny their pain. Later in the process I began to understand what part of me was reaching toward this subject and what relevance it had to my life.

My relationship with my father was one that I would describe as deeply close, connected in a very profound way. In retrospect, I understand that our closeness was not always healthy, that I idealized my father in order to quiet my fears about the sides of him that scared me, and that our closeness isolated me from other members of my family. But at the time, I felt both blessed and indentured by his love and I never questioned beyond that. We were, he used to say, "cut from the same cloth." We understood each other's insides, we liked the same foods, we walked together, drank café-au-lait in the sun and discussed great subjects.

I never remember not being taken seriously by him when he was sober. The thoughts I expressed seemed always to be of interest. In his presence, I felt that the world was on my side. My father began to drink when I was a little girl. Liquor began to erode the father I knew by around my fourth-grade year—slowly at first, then more each week. By the time I was in the sixth grade, the father I had known was available only, say, 30 percent of the time. The other 70 percent, he was lost in a world that belonged more to alcohol than to me or the family or his community. Slowly, "the drink took the man." I watched my father die a little more each day, like seeing someone drown in a deep lake and not being able to bring the person out. It was as if our family dynamic was frozen in place at that point in time. The sheer pain of it all left us in stupefied silence, traumatized, eerily still, removed and out of sync with the world around us, like an untimely frost on October leaves. We were out of season. Life was losing its predictable order. Nothing worked—not treatment, prayer, being good, being tough, being perfect, being outrageous. Nothing helped.

As the father we knew died, my family died too. Each day we were a little sadder, and each day we grew more and more adept at hiding that sadness. Because of our traumatized reactions, we could not share our sorrow and confusion, and relationships that had once been easy became tense. We took our pain out on each other because we didn't know how to process it as a family. Early on I withdrew into myself. Because what went on around me was confusing and the very people I had previously gone to for support were now less available, I numbed out emotionally, going through the motions of what used to be my life without much feeling attached. I didn't cry. Consequently, I got migraine headaches, stomach distress and heart pains, but none of them, I told myself, were all that bad.

One day at school, in my 11th-grade year, I felt a migraine coming on. I went to the school nurse to ask to be sent home. She asked me some questions about my life and I reluctantly explained my situation at home, to which she said, "You're going to hate me today, but some day you will thank me. You can't go home." Instead, she gave me water, aspirin, a bed and a blanket. I can still see that little room and feel the itchiness of the institutional blanket drawn across my legs. I remember staring at the ceiling. She told me that what was happening to my father and my family was truly sad, tragic even, and that it was normal to be sad about it. I hadn't heard that till that moment. I think many people had said it, but I hadn't heard it. I felt tears move down my cheeks, almost imperceptibly—disconnected little drops of water running along the sides of my face. Then I did something I hadn't done in a long time—I let myself cry. I lay there and cried all the tears I had bottled up for my lost life. What had happened to us? Where had we gone? I was embarrassed by the stifled little moans I heard coming from me, but the tears kept flowing. I could feel my stomach heave and rumble, but still they kept coming. The room seemed as if it were spinning through space. My head felt as though a truck were driving through it; I was disoriented and self-conscious but my body kept crying in spite of me. After I had cried for what seemed like hours, the nurse let me choose whether to go home or not. I chose to stay. I took a walk, had a cup of coffee, pulled myself together and walked back into my life. Somehow that crying, that acknowledgment of pain and loss, allowed me to reenter both my life and my self. I have never really left since.

What that school nurse taught me was that I had to grieve. I had to face my life to stay in it, and in order to do that I had to grieve what was no longer there. I began to write at that point in my life. When I felt sad, I used to go into the stationery store and mentally talk to the neatly stacked legal pads and blank paper lined up along the open shelves. They held my feelings for me; their very blankness drew thoughts and images from my mind and calmed my spirit. I now know that giving into the grief—*sitting in the wound*—allowed me to restore my life again. Once I could sit in my own life rather than deny it, I could assess it realistically. I got a job, I spent time with friends I genuinely enjoyed, I developed a couple outside interests, I started going to church and joined the choir. I was amazed at how much the world had to offer me if I let it, and that feeling has never really left me. The shell around my heart cracked and the world came in.

Today I understand that surrendering to a process of mourning, however awkward, allowed me to take in life again. That process has returned to me all that I lost and much more. My husband and I are celebrating our 23rd wedding anniversary, and we have a son and daughter whom we adore and who love us. These relationships at times have felt almost magical in their capacity to bring beauty into my life. My husband and I work constantly on our marriage, getting the help we need to plow through old wounds that could drive us apart and using them instead as indicators of where our work lies. My siblings and mother and I have been able to share our hurt and reach for each other again in ways that feel safe and nurturing, to enjoy each other's company and accept each other's love and support. I am able today to appreciate what a wonderful family I came from and how much I was given by them. We were all just doing the best we could with what we had to work with at the time, and we have all come to realize that what we have is far more than what we lost. I feel so deeply grateful today for the family I came from and the family I married into.

This process works. It is time-honored, built into our biology. The natural healing system built into the human being is a way to release pain and stress. This, I am convinced, is what is underneath violence, epidemic depression and social alienation. It is unfelt, unprocessed pain that fuels pathology and acting out much of the time. Great religions have rituals tailored to meet just these human needs. In today's mobile society, with its longer life span and decreased extended family, we need to return to these old rituals and revitalize our existing institutions. We need to develop new institutions to find ways of having support and community, and rites of passage in our lengthened stages of life. We need to expand our idea of grief and mourning, extending it from death into life. Each life trauma or loss needs to be mourned and processed to whatever extent is appropriate in order to integrate it and move on.

When people with unresolved grief and pain from the past enter into intimate adult relationships, they bring their pain with them. The very intimacy, the feelings of dependency and need that are part of any intimate relationship, triggers buried fears and hurts. Conflicts that would otherwise be resolved with a little work trigger unresolved conflicts from the past, and in a split second the past and present become an indistinguishable muddle of emotion. Soon the full force of the old pain gets acted out in the present, projected onto the screen of the relationship—not the one that caused it but the one that triggered it.

The Four Stages of Grief

People who experience loss pass through a predictable set of feelings or stages. Though these stages may be experienced simultaneously, repeated or leapfrogged, and may be short or long in duration, they provide a useful map of the emotional terrain more or less crossed after a loss.

The stages we pass through as a consequence of loss and separation, according to British psychoanalyst John Bowlby, are (1) numbness, (2) yearning and searching, (3) disorganization, anger, despair, and (4) reorganization. *Numbness* is that sort of nonexperience of shutting down emotionally and psychologically—walking through the day as if anesthetized, seeing the world moving along but feeling estranged and disconnected from it. *Yearning and searching* refer to that ache that can sometimes seem physically located somewhere in the chest. It is a longing, even at times an unbearable feeling of unrequited needing and inner or outer searching for what feels missing. It can be accompanied by searching behavior ranging from real searching for what is lost, to looking to replace lost love in functional and not so functional ways. *Disorganization, anger* and *despair* are the natural outcome of searching and not finding, yearning for what feels painfully absent. We can feel an irrational anger, even rage, over what is missing. We despair over the prospect of never getting it and are not able to organize either thought or day while carrying around this throbbing emotional and psychological wound. *Reorganization/integration* is a natural outcome of spent grief, of coming to a point of acceptance over what is lost. Grieving actually allows reorganization and integration to happen because the pain is experienced rather than repressed, and so can be integrated into the self-system rather than split off. This is the stage of coming to terms with the loss and finding meaning in life again, incorporating what has been learned from the experience into our personal story.

The Four Stages of
Grieving and Mourning

I. Numbness

Description: This is a period of emotional numbness. Trauma survivors know something happened but their feelings are shut down and out of reach. They may try to deny the extent of the impact of the loss in an effort to make it feel less threatening and more manageable. Emotional numbness or shutdown, if unresolved, can become a part of the operating organization of the self, impairing a person's ability to be deeply intimate or to interact with people and situations in a spontaneous and attuned manner. It can create what appears to be rigidity or dullness in the personality. A person who is numb or shut down has difficulty being emotionally spontaneous and present in a relationship.

Inner thoughts and emotions: It didn't happen. It's not that bad. This isn't my life. It's all a bad dream.

Consequences of not working through this stage: If trauma survivors do not successfully work through this stage, they can shut down a part of themselves, becoming emotionally numb and unavailable for deep feeling on a consistent basis. Deep connection or feeling may occur sporadically, but maintaining a connection with this deeper part of self or a deep connection with others can feel threatening. Spontaneity may be undermined, and people who have not worked through this stage can seem rigid or unable to react easily and appropriately in the here and now. They may have difficulty identifying what they are feeling and communicating that to another person they are in relationship with because their feelings are somewhat of a mystery to them. They tend to deny, repress, ignore or skip over their true emotional response so quickly and automatically that they can't feel this feeling and identify it. Rather, their reactions may take on either a staged quality (i.e., "What should I be feeling now?") or a wooden quality showing little affect. Emotional numbness leaves a person "going through the motions" with little feeling attached.

II. Yearning and Searching

Description: This stage is marked by a yearning for the lost object (person, situation) and searching for it in other people, places and things. *Ghosting* or the sense of a continuing presence of the lost object may be experienced. There is a deep yearning for what was lost—be it a stage of life, a part of the self or a person—followed by a searching for a way to replace the lost experience. In this period, trauma survivors are at risk for rebound relationships and rash attempts to "replace" what was lost rather than process and integrate the loss. At this stage, it is easy to trade one relationship for another on the rebound. The unresolved yearning can leave someone literally going through life trying to replace what was lost in childhood, adolescence or adulthood, or in the case of abstinence from addiction to drugs and alcohol, replacing the lost drugs and alcohol with food, sex or compulsive activity. When trauma survivors lose their self-medication of drugs and alcohol, they need to enter an active program of emotional recovery to resolve their emotional wounds so that they do not either relapse into drugs and alcohol or trade one addiction for another.

Inner thoughts and emotions: If only I had done something differently. I would give anything for it to be the way it was. Where am I? What's going on? Everything feels different. Where is my life?

Consequences of not working through this stage: People who have not successfully worked through this stage of the grief process are at risk for spending their lives searching to replace what they feel they lost, "looking for love in all the wrong places." Yearning and searching for what was lost (while not consciously grieving it) can leave these people feeling as if they have a hole inside them that cannot be filled, a thirst that cannot be quenched or a question that cannot be answered. They may find an experience or a person that temporarily relieves this deep longing, but unless the original loss is made conscious, grieved and understood, the solution will be a momentary one. The unfelt wound will reassert itself, making the current solution feel inadequate and wanting. This is different from a human existential yearning. Yearning from an unresolved grief wound throbs beneath the membrane of current experience

©1997 Tian Dayton, *Heartwounds*, adapted from John Bowlby

meant to keep pain at bay. This is a yearning that needs to be understood for what it is, connected to what it is really about and integrated into the self-system.

III. Disorganization, Anger and Despair

Description: In this stage, trauma survivors are disillusioned. Life did not happen as they planned. They have feelings of anger, despair and disappointment that come and go and are overwhelming at times. Their lives can feel as though they no longer belong to them. Normal routines are disrupted, which can make them feel lost and disconnected from the life they're used to. Lack of resolution of this stage can lead to depression and an inability to move through life in an organized manner. They may become hypervigilant in an attempt to keep perceived pain at bay, or avoid situations that arouse or put them in touch with the anger and despair that lie buried within them, which they may wish unconsciously to deny. It is difficult for people lost in this stage to trust a relationship or to have the faith that if they allow themselves to be intimate and depend on someone, it will not ultimately lead only to more loss and disappointment.

Inner thoughts and emotions: Nothing I can do will make it better. How can I go on the same way? I'm afraid of my own life, of my future. I'll never get over this. I'm so angry.

Consequences of not working through this stage: When people do not work through the stages of disruption, anger and despair, they can go through life feeling they got a "raw deal." They may have inappropriate displays of anger, or they may turn the anger inward on themselves and become depressed; they may develop a negative attitude toward life. They may find that they have trouble organizing and taking methodical steps on their life path or sustaining a healthy relationship because their unresolved grief has left them hanging in a psychologically and emotionally disorganized internal state. When someone is stuck in unresolved anger, it can seriously undermine both intimate and professional relationships. The "free-floating" anger will seek periodic relief and may express itself at the expense of current life circumstances, making the person feel life is unmanageable and overwhelming.

©1997 Tian Dayton, *Heartwounds,* adapted from John Bowlby

That anger will need to be connected to its origins so that it can be worked through in a real and meaningful way; *then* it can be deactivated within the self, freeing a person from its powerful grip.

IV. Reorganization/Integration

Description: In this stage, trauma survivors call their loss by its right name. They begin accepting the reality of their situation and along with it, the emotional pain they know it inevitably brings. They accept feelings of disruption, sadness, yearning and fear as part of the loss. They alternately struggle with and accept their feelings of disorientation, or their sense of being cheated or tricked. They come to terms with their powerlessness over the situation and restore their emotional and psychological equilibrium. They begin to put the loss into perspective, to reenter their lives and re-engage in their own activities and plans. They begin to integrate the effects of the loss into their sense of who they are and what life contains.

Inner thoughts and emotions: Life has ups and downs; it has losses. I'm not immune to life's problems. Life still has something to offer me. My life feels sort of different and sort of the same.

Consequences of not working through this stage: When someone does not work through the stage of reorganization and integration, the loss does not get fully resolved and reintegrated into the self-system. Personal history is lost, and old losses are banished to hidden regions of the mind and heart. What was bad does not get released, and what was good does not get preserved. Trauma victims can only deeply and fully reinvent themselves when they have enough pieces of self with which to work. Reinventing half of ourselves means just that. Moving successfully through losses and transitions impels us to move from disorganization to reorganization, using life problems as grist for the mill of personal change and growth. This enables us to pull wisdom and meaning from pain, which deepens and strengthens our relationship with self and our resilience in living.

Grief Triggers

Anniversary reactions: Anniversary reactions are common on or around the anniversary of a loss or death. One may feel a vague or even an overwhelming sense of pain related to a loss that feels as if it is coming out of nowhere. This reaction may also be experienced around previous significant dates such as hospitalization, sickness, sobriety or divorce.

Holiday reactions: Holidays often stimulate pain from previous losses. Because they are traditional ritual gatherings, they heighten our awareness about what is missing or what has changed.

Age-correspondence reactions: This reaction occurs when, for example, a child reaches the age at which there was a loss by someone he or she identified with. A daughter whose mother divorced around age 45 may find herself thinking about or even considering divorce when she reaches that approximate age.

Seasonal reactions: Change of seasons can stimulate grief or be unconsciously associated with a loss, thus causing a type of depression during a particular season.

Music-stimulated grief: Music can act as a doorway to the unconscious. It activates the right brain, drawing out associations and feelings that get stimulated by a particular song or music.

Ritual-stimulated grief: Important shared rituals can stimulate grief when there has been a loss. For example, family dinners or Sunday brunch can be a sad time for family members who have experienced divorce.

Signs and Symptoms: Other Ways in Which Grief Can Manifest

Memorialization: Loss needs to be consciously memorialized through open communal sharing or ritual so that it does not get lived out unconsciously in a repetition compulsion, repeating an unresolved loss by re-creating the painful circumstance over and over in life.

Mummification: In this form of extended grieving, the griever unnaturally preserves objects or parts of a house as they were at the time of the loss.

Self-mutilation: Self-mutilation can be a direct result of unresolved grief. Anger, despair, disorganization and fragmentation are managed by cutting and damaging the self rather than in a healthy and open manner. Cutters gain some sense of control over their disintegrating inner world by taking their pain out in a controlled, masochistic fashion, and the sight of blood may serve to bring cutters from their dissociated world back to the present.

Ghosting: Ghosting is the phenomenon of imagining you are seeing the lost person where the person is not present. This may be caused, in part, by a heightened "perceptual set" as a result of unconscious or conscious yearning for the lost person or objects. Visual signals may be interpreted by the brain as a reminder or perceived match for the lost person. For example, someone who possesses features similar to the person who has been lost can be momentarily mistaken for that person by the griever in a quick flash, triggering a grief memory or association.

Survival guilt: This refers to the guilt carried if one person survives a situation when others do not. It can also be felt by a person who recovers from a dysfunctional family pattern in which other family members continue to be mired.

Anticipatory grief: This is grief in anticipation of a feared event or loss. It is feeling grief before an anticipated loss has occurred. Anticipatory grief is natural and would only be considered problematic if it seriously interfered with normal life functioning.

Caretaking: Caretaking occurs when a person displaces anxiety and worry onto another person, becoming obsessed with another's problems rather than owning their own unresolved pain.

Sudden outbursts of anger: Sudden outbursts of anger that are inappropriately large, given the situation, may be a sign of unresolved grief.

Emotional numbness: Emotional numbness or shutdown can be the result of unresolved grief. It is experienced as a rather flat, unexpressive affect within the person and in their responses to others.

Inadequate Attempts at Dealing with Grief

Premature resolution: This occurs when people try to force themselves to resolve grief without allowing themselves to move through the full cycle of mourning. In these cases, the unresolved feelings tend to come out sideways in the form of projections, transferences, bursts of anger, bouts of depression and so on.

Pseudo-resolution: Pseudo-resolution is a false resolution that occurs when a person fools himself or herself into feeling that mourning has been resolved, when it actually has not taken place sufficiently.

Replacement: This refers to the person who replaces the loss rather than processing the feelings around it. For example, the divorced person who immediately marries again may feel he or she has solved the pain of loss when, in fact, the loss has not been processed and learned from. The same issues that led to one loss tend to reappear in the next relationship.

Displacement: This occurs when mourners cannot connect their pain to what is actually causing it and instead displace the grief, upset, anger and sadness onto something or someone else, thus *displacing* the pain where it does not belong. It is therefore difficult to resolve the grief because it is felt around the wrong subject and needs to be consciously linked back to what is actually causing it.

Warning Signs of Unresolved Grief

1. Excessive guilt

2. Excessive anger/sudden angry outbursts

3. Recurring or long-lasting depression

4. Caretaking behavior

5. Self-mutilation

6. Emotional numbness or constriction

©1997 Tian Dayton, *Heartwounds*

Warning Signs of Unresolved Trauma

1. Risk-taking behavior

2. Desire to self-medicate with alcohol or drugs

3. Chronic or recurring depression or feelings of despair

4. Emotional constriction/lack of affect and spontaneity

5. Drive to re-create painful emotional dynamics

6. Loss of ability to modulate emotion

7. Inability to take in support

8. Psychosomatic symptoms

9. Hypervigilance

PART II

The Effect of Trauma on the Personality

Aloys Wach

The Resonance of Traum

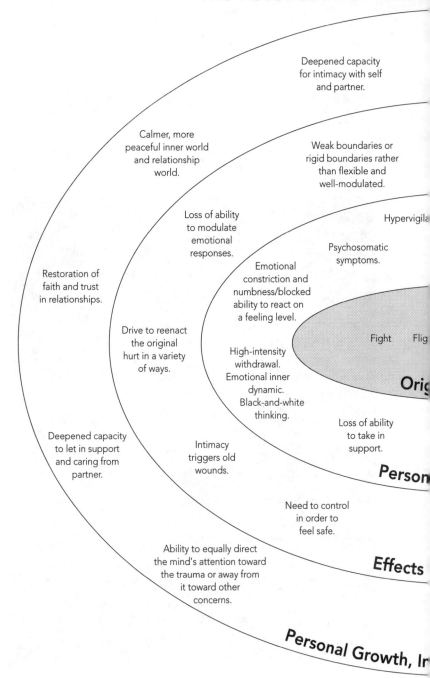

Deepened capacity for intimacy with self and partner.

Calmer, more peaceful inner world and relationship world.

Weak boundaries or rigid boundaries rather than flexible and well-modulated.

Loss of ability to modulate emotional responses.

Hypervigila

Psychosomatic symptoms.

Emotional constriction and numbness/blocked ability to react on a feeling level.

Restoration of faith and trust in relationships.

Drive to reenact the original hurt in a variety of ways.

High-intensity withdrawal. Emotional inner dynamic. Black-and-white thinking.

Fight   Flig

Orig

Deepened capacity to let in support and caring from partner.

Intimacy triggers old wounds.

Loss of ability to take in support.

Person

Need to control in order to feel safe.

Effects

Ability to equally direct the mind's attention toward the trauma or away from it toward other concerns.

Personal Growth, In

om Hurt to Healing

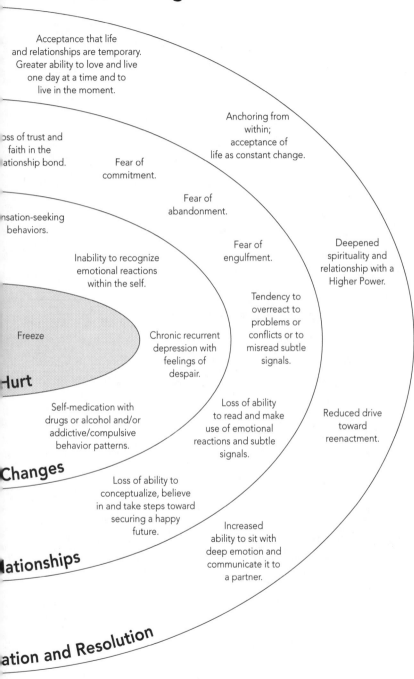

Acceptance that life and relationships are temporary. Greater ability to love and live one day at a time and to live in the moment.

Anchoring from within; acceptance of life as constant change.

ɔss of trust and faith in the ʌationship bond.

Fear of commitment.

Fear of abandonment.

nsation-seeking behaviors.

Inability to recognize emotional reactions within the self.

Fear of engulfment.

Deepened spirituality and relationship with a Higher Power.

Tendency to overreact to problems or conflicts or to misread subtle signals.

Freeze

Chronic recurrent depression with feelings of despair.

Hurt

Self-medication with drugs or alcohol and/or addictive/compulsive behavior patterns.

Loss of ability to read and make use of emotional reactions and subtle signals.

Reduced drive toward reenactment.

Changes

Loss of ability to conceptualize, believe in and take steps toward securing a happy future.

Increased ability to sit with deep emotion and communicate it to a partner.

lationships

ation and Resolution

rtwounds

Give sorrow words; the grief that does not speak
Whispers to the o'er-fraught heart, and bids it break.

Shakespeare, *Macbeth*

Let mourning stop when one's
grief is fully expressed.

Confucius

There is no doubt that sorrow brings
one down in the world. The aristocratic privilege of
silence belongs, you soon find out, to only the
happy state or, at least, to the state when
pain keeps within bounds.

Elizabeth Brown

Grief even in a child hates the light
and shrinks from human eyes.

Thomas de Quincey,
The Affliction of Childhood,
Suspiria de Profundis

Every childhood's conflictual experiences
remain hidden and locked in darkness, and the key
to our understanding the life that follows
is hidden away with them.

Alice Miller,
The Drama of the Gifted Child

The Effect of Trauma
on the Personality

*What loneliness is more lonely
than mistrust?*

GEORGE ELIOT

Meet Connie and Bill. They have just arrived home from work within an hour of each other. Connie is a dental hygienist, Bill a computer programmer. They have a three-year-old daughter, Lizzie, and want to be the best parents they can be; to give Lizzie the childhood they wish they had had. But it's hard. When Connie arrives home, Lizzie needs attention, so dinner doesn't get started. Lizzie is tired and needs her mother's time. Connie is tired too, but nevertheless, she does her best. Connie feels a little guilty for being gone all day. Lizzie is the light of her life—but Connie's back and feet still ache.

Next, Bill arrives home. He is late because computers just don't seem to break down on a family-friendly schedule. Bill is tired. He is also hungry. When he arrives, Connie wants him to take over with Lizzie so she can start dinner—or he could start dinner while she attends Lizzie—but he always makes a mess and takes longer. Connie wonders how her mother did it with four kids. Bill wonders how it would feel to come home to dinner made and no expectations of "chipping in." But that apparently doesn't work that well either, since both their parents' marriages ended up in divorce. Connie is wondering if this is how her mother felt at times like these and what that means about her marriage. Bill is starting to wish he had taken longer to fix that computer. They both wonder how their parents would have handled these feelings. Then, they quickly remember that whatever their parents did obviously didn't work anyway. They wonder what the experts would say they should do, then they remember they didn't get to the chapter on this—whatever this is.

Soon, Connie starts seeing Bill as a pain in the neck—without him she and Lizzie could eat scrambled eggs and bond in front of *Snow White and the Seven Dwarfs*. Bill is beginning to see Connie as self-centered, never interested in his day. Before they know it, they are snapping at each other. Just a little bit at first, but somehow they go from 1 to 10 in a matter of minutes, and now they are feeling about the same age as Lizzie and saying things to each other that they would be embarrassed by if anyone overheard, trading insult for insult, injury for injury. Soon Lizzie is crying, Connie is crying and Bill is yelling. Feelings are erupting that have little to do with what is going on in this situation but that have been building up over time. These feelings carry with them all the power of old hurts from the past, from relationships and situations that never quite got resolved. Words that each of them hunger to say get said here, whether or not "here" is the right place to say them. What, they wonder, is going on, and how did they get here . . . again?

When couples interact, they interact with their child selves and their adolescent selves as well as their adult selves. Trauma freezes moments in time. If, for example, a daughter was traumatized by a father's yelling, that scene can replay in her mind if her husband yells at her. When she was yelled at as a child, she was a little girl being chastised by a grown man. She may have felt helpless, humiliated and hurt. When her husband yells at her, even though she is now a wife and a woman of five-feet-eight inches, she may *feel* like a small, defenseless child. Conversely, when a son was being criticized by a mother, he was three-feet tall and his mother seemed like a giant. Later, when his wife criticizes him, he may return to feeling like a bad boy, small, dependent and unable to speak up for himself. A similar phenomenon can occur in other relationships. For example, an employer's unrealistically high expectations or critical manner can trigger these same reactions, returning the victim of trauma to a childlike state of feeling fearful or helpless. This can, in turn, make the employee wish to please, placate, withdraw, rebel; that is, the person will use the defenses that he or she used as a child in order to stay safe.

Because trauma is in essence a wound in the attachment or relationship bond, the symptoms associated with having been traumatized evidence themselves in relationships.

I'm Okay, You Need Therapy: Mourning and Misappropriation

When we deny an old hurt, say from childhood, that needs grieving, we risk confusing old hurts with new ones, which can make the new ones feel overwhelming and unmanageable. The unfelt wound cries out in the darkness of the psyche to be known. It lies dormant but not deactivated within the self-system, an emotional bomb waiting to explode, waiting for the right person or relationship to trigger it. Once it is triggered, it gets directed at whomever or whatever acted as the trigger, and for a moment the wound is given voice—not the right voice perhaps, but the only voice in which it knows how to speak.

The child who was "alone in the presence of the mother," finds a place to shed his tears, as Dr. D. W. Winnicott includes in his seminal research on mother-child relationships. The child, now the man, seeks an expression, albeit convoluted, for the ungrieved wound he carries within himself. Until it is grieved and understood for what it is, he may project his emotional dilemma onto his partner in the form of blame, anger and criticism. Additionally, he may himself experience disagreement as criticism or conflict as abuse. He may misread signals from his partner because his protective radar is set too high. The child in him who was traumatized by what he experienced as udisinterest, neglect or abandonment will stand in rigid hypervigilance to keep pain away. Just as a bruise will be tender to the physical touch, an ungrieved emotional wound will be tender to the emotional touch. The degree of self-protection is equal to the severity of the wound, whether it be to the heart or to the hand.

When we neglect genuine wounds to the heart, those old hurts assert themselves in the dynamics of our intimate relationships. We create a house of mirrors in which we see ourselves reflected back to us in a variety of distorted shapes—the shapes we see are the parts of us that lay hidden within the self, manipulated into silence. Hence we do not get a clear and honest reflection of who we are on the inside. We fight rather than talk, blame rather than own, and alternate between attacking and withdrawing.

People who have been traumatized—whether from sexual or physical abuse, parental neglect, being left by a loved one, random violence or divorce—walk away from the experience feeling a loss of innocence. Their ideals have been shattered, their trust violated. It is hard to heal this wound because it cuts so deep. That young and vulnerable part of us can feel dropped, by life, by the person we relied on or even by God. It can be difficult to go to this place within ourselves and let the pain come out. It is too well-guarded and too threatening to own this loss of innocence, this rupture of faith and hope—this broken dream. But it is the tears shed from this brokenness and the rage hurling from this wound that have the power to heal it. We need to go there, call it by its right name and provide a safe place for these feelings to emerge. Then, we must introduce corrective experiences so that what was dropped can be held, and what was broken can be reconnected.

Describing the Wound: What Do We Mean by Trauma and How Does It Impact the Way We See the World?

Lindemann, in his penetrating research on the subject, defines trauma as the "sudden, uncontrollable disruption of affiliative bonds." Childhood trauma has a profound impact because uncontrollable and frightening experiences may have their strongest effect when the central nervous system and cognitive functioning are not yet fully developed. A child copes with trauma with the tools available at that particular stage of maturity—seeing and interpreting the meaning of a situation through the lens and reasoning of a child's mind. Children make meaning out of traumatic circumstances and live by their perceptions as absolute truth. They carry these interpretations into adult relationships. Children who are abused may become adults who feel that they deserve mistreatment. Children who are neglected may become adults who cannot connect easily. Children of divorce may fear they cannot sustain a relationship. When, as adults, their old pain gets triggered, they freeze like deer in the headlights and fall back on the defenses that they used as children. Let's now examine some of the defenses used by children when they are overwhelmed by a life circumstance.

Splitting—seeing someone as alternately all good or all bad—is a primitive defense in very young children who are unable to make sense of overwhelmingly painful or traumatic circumstances. The children cannot integrate the manner in which a parent is acting. The actions of the parent are too inconsistent. Perhaps the parent is solicitous and attentive on the one hand, then rageful or abusive on the other; or the parent may display the Jekyll and Hyde personality so typical of an alcoholic. Later in life, when as adults their partners trigger them, these now-grown children might react by seeing their partner as completely wrong and bad, and they will temporarily forget all the positive aspects of the relationship. For example, Giermo "splits" in relationships with women, which we will see in an upcoming case study. When he and his partner are engaged in an intense conflict, rather than seeing the conflict as a *part* of the relationship, he sees it as *all* of the relationship. He temporarily loses his ability to place the conflict in the context of the overall relationship and becomes overwhelmed and desperate. He forgets that his partner has many sides, and sees only what is threatening and problematic. Though all people do this to some extent, victims of trauma are especially prone to catastrophizing relationship dynamics that trigger old fears and anxieties. Obviously this makes it difficult to keep problems in their proper perspective and to work through them.

Another common childhood defense is *dissociation*. Jeff, a member of our therapy group represented in this book, learned to dissociate from the emotional pain he felt at being ignored and verbally abused by his father. As a small boy he sat wide-eyed and motionless through his father's drunken verbal lashings. When the pain of his father's disgust became too great, he took the only route available to him as a child who was not allowed to talk back or run away: He ran away inside of himself by disappearing into a world of daydreams and fantasies; he dissociated.

As an adult, he still dissociates when he feels emotional pain. It has become such a habit of mind that he now has trouble even identifying what he is feeling and putting it into words. This keeps him from being able to communicate his needs to another person so that they can be known and talked over.

Dissociating is a defense against pain or perceived danger— Jeff remained physically present, but psychologically he flew away. This is a common defense against physical or sexual abuse when a child has no other way out.

Still another defense is to become *numb*, to be in the situation but to *shut down* our emotional response to it. A group participant named James reverted to shutting down and numbing his feelings as a child. He, like Jeff, was rejected and ridiculed by his father, who held him to impossibly high standards that, even when he reached them, did not keep him safe from his father's humiliation and anger. He was forced to stay in the room while his father let loose on him in the form of criticism and yelling, and was roundly disciplined when he attempted to defend himself in any way. Consequently, he learned to numb out his emotional response, which over time turned into shutting down any intense emotional response almost involuntarily. Though this preserved his sanity as a young man, it left him unable to respond spontaneously or authentically in relationships. Now he protects himself even where it is not necessary because numbness has become a part of his personality.

A fourth tool of defense in the mind of a child is *idealization*. As a child, Connie responded to her father by idealizing him. She adored him and managed her fear of his anger and inconsistent behavior by, in a sense, pretending they weren't there, and by making his good qualities so wonderful that they could assuage her fear of his bad ones. Actually, her need to do this speaks to how much his anger and inconsistent behavior frightened her. Had her mother been able to help her understand and put her father into perspective, Connie could have leaned on her mother for support and comfort and reduced her fear and need to idealize. Sadly, her mother felt as frightened as Connie was and could offer no such respite from anxiety.

Though all of these defenses serve to help the child maintain some sense of harmony, the harmony is had at the expense of feelings that are authentic. Generally, a person employs more than one defense. The defenses then become a part of the personality, where they intertwine themselves around the development and organization of the whole personality and get carried into adult relationships.

Later in life, "victims of trauma may gain some sense of control by avoiding intimate relationships because they unconsciously fear another violation of the attachment bond. However, avoiding relationships further isolates the person and deepens their sense of life feeling meaningless which perpetuates the central role of the trauma" (van der Kolk, 1987). Children who dissociated may dissociate in adult relationships when in the stress of conflict. They may disappear into themselves, remaining physically present but psychologically and emotionally absent. Children who numbed out or shut down may use these same defenses in adult relationships when they feel hurt or vulnerable, withdrawing into themselves and losing access to their own feelings and the possibility of communicating them to their partner. Children who split may become adults who get lost in their own intense feeling state and may overreact to conflict and imagine the person they are with transforming before their eyes into all that they fear an intimate partner can become.

The Disorganized Inner World

After experiencing trauma, survivors' thought processes become disorganized and their inner world is increasingly preoccupied with emotions related to the trauma. Later, as adults, they tend to respond to feelings triggered by intimacy in seemingly paradoxical ways by shutting down, or with the intensity of emotion appropriate to the original trauma. This is the classic black-and-white type of thinking. It is an alternating of both numbing and intense re-experiencing; thus the trauma dominates the mental life of the victim long after the original experience.

One syndrome that can include any or all of these defenses is Post-Traumatic Stress Disorder (PTSD). Though this diagnosis was originally employed to describe trauma as the result of war, it is now widely used to name a cluster of characteristics exhibited by people with wide-ranging types of trauma, from war to natural disaster to family abuse, divorce, addiction or neglect. These characteristics exist on a continuum. Wherever a person falls on that continuum defines the extent of impact trauma has had on the personality. Some people cope better than others, depending on their biological setup, the supports available to them at the time of the trauma, along with their stage of development and how they witnessed others coping with the stress.

A vicious circle ensues because some of the most effective ways of gaining relief from acute stress are lost to the victim of trauma. "People with PTSD lose their capacity to symbolize, fantasize and sublimate as a way of anticipating and modifying emotional responses" (van der Kolk, 1987). Play and fantasy can feel chaotic and out of control for survivors of trauma, who have learned that the world around them can suddenly change. The spontaneity and unpredictability of play and fantasy can feel threatening to survivors, who may be wired to overreact to intense stimuli, inhibiting their ability to use their imagination and fantasy to transform the "small injuries of daily life" and make them feel acceptable. "Hence they are deprived of precisely the psychological mechanisms that allow others to cope with these small injuries of daily life. This lack of tolerance interferes with their ability to grieve and work through ordinary conflicts and thus limits their capacity to accumulate restitutive and gratifying experiences. The result is a robot-like existence, devoid of fantasy and sympathy for others, often accompanied by chronic physical illness, alcoholism, or drug dependence." (van der Kolk, 1987)

We saw this clearly in soldiers returning from the Vietnam War. I think we see it today in inner-city children, children from broken homes or homes where addiction, divorce or abuse is present, and victims of tragedies and natural disasters. Without a process of grief to let go of the pain attached to a loss or trauma, they are blocked in their emotional life. Inner peace needs to be restored through a process of grieving. Then the internal world can once again open enough to embrace and trust experiences that feel good. Without this resolution of the trauma, survivors remain hypervigilant, and intimacy feels frightening because the feelings of closeness, vulnerability and dependency can trigger an unconscious fear of reexperiencing pain associated with lost attachment bonds. The unconscious feeling is, "If I let this feel good and come to depend on it and enjoy it, it will lead to pain." This gives way to trauma survivors' distorted conclusion that they can protect themselves by not letting themselves feel love or dependency. The trauma survivors' inability to "accumulate restitutive and gratifying experiences" underscores the need for grief work to be fully undertaken so that the beauty, intimacy and pleasures of life can once again be absorbed. Trauma dominates the survivor's inner world. Traumatic memories cannot be avoided. Even when they have been pushed out of consciousness, they return in the form of reenactments, nightmares and intense feelings related to the trauma.

It is not only the intensity of the traumatic experience that defines its impact on the survivor's inner world but the *meaning* that the person experiencing it made of it at the time. For example, a child who is verbally or physically abused by a drunk parent will cope with the emotional and psychological skills that he or she possesses at that developmental moment. A young child does not have the capacity to think, "My parent has been drinking; I can't take what they say or do seriously." Rather, the child will try to make sense of the absurd—using the child's own meaning as a way of coping with a situation he or she does not understand. Generally, children will believe what they are told by their parents—that they are bad, that if only they would behave, get better grades or do what is being demanded of them, their parents would not act this way. Children may believe that their parents are only rageful and critical because they have disappointed them in some way, that they are bad children. As a result, abused children can carry an oblique sense of shame and failure that gets played out later in adult relationships.

Trauma, Self-Medication and Addiction

Self-medicating is a direct reaction to trauma. When children or adults are deeply wounded, they cope as we have discussed with the tools available to them at the time. Unfortunately, some of the most readily available tools in our society are drugs and alcohol. Drugs and alcohol take the pain away. For the teenager or adult who is in emotional pain, drugs and alcohol appear to be a way out of that pain—and so begins a lifelong battle with addiction. Sadly, the very commodity that supplies immediate relief takes on a life of its own. What began as an attempt to solve or lessen pain becomes a source of anguish and pain in and of itself. Tolerance increases, and soon more drugs and more alcohol are needed to manage emotional pain, and the person taking them slips into a continued and growing need for chemicals.

The recovery process requires addicts to revisit the emotional pain that they drown out with chemicals. When addicts become sober, the self-medication is removed but the emotional pain is still there. This is why unless this pain is processed and worked through, addicts may either switch to a different addiction, such as food, sex or work, or they may relapse and go back to using drugs and alcohol. Unresolved trauma and grief need to be worked through for addicts to become not only physically but emotionally sober, in charge of their own inner world and able to experience deep feelings, understand them and talk about them rather than act them out in self-destructive ways.

How Drugs Interrupt the Mourning Process

Giermo's losses were numerous. Early in his life, at age two, his parents emigrated from South America to work and settle in the United States, leaving him with his paternal grandmother. The psychodrama we played out in group in relation to them was a memory about reuniting with his mother after over a year's absence. There was his adored mother standing in the room where he was to see her again. He stood at the door, transfixed, frozen. The mother he thought had abandoned him was standing like a goddess before his eyes. He could not move, he was so shocked to see her. She scooped up her other children while he stood watching, unable to break his pose and move toward her. No one thought to explain his mother's absence to him in a way that he could understand and no one, including himself, realized how traumatized he was at this prolonged separation from her. His separation constituted an interruption of the affiliative bond at a crucial moment in his developmental need for her, the fallout from which was a mistrust of women. His paternal grandmother was a harsh woman who was not a suitable surrogate for the mother he adored.

However, even reuniting with his mother did not fully heal the rift because, in his child mind, she might leave again at any moment. The family moved to the United States, and he now faced adjusting to a new country and what felt to him like a new mother. At this point, pleasing his parents was of paramount importance to him. He had made his own childlike meaning out of his parents' absence. He had displeased them in some way, they no longer wanted him, and therefore they had left him as a sort of punishment with a grandmother he barely new. Now, in order to keep this from happening again, he must be very good, he must anticipate his parents' needs and wishes before they became a problem and keep them happy no matter what.

As time went on, the ethic of machismo in his culture made him feel that he should bear up to pain like a man, burying any anxiety or hurt feelings beneath a mask of toughness and invulnerability. If Giermo brought home a B+, he was beaten because it wasn't an A. During the entire systematic beating with a belt, the father would say, "I am only doing this because I love you." Giermo came to pride himself on not crying or letting his father see his pain. Love and pain became fused in Giermo's mind. He was forced to accept the beatings; after all, working for an A was better than being abandoned again, and he tried to improve himself. Perhaps an A next time would please his father. He could help his mother more around the house or with his younger brother. He would do better in athletics.

Eventually, in spite of Giermo's best efforts, his father left the mother and children. Giermo, of course, thought he had been unworthy of his staying, wondering without ever saying it what he might have done differently to make him want to stay. To complicate matters further, his father sat his three sons down and asked them if they wanted him to leave, a decision no hurting child should be called upon to make. They all said yes and lived thereafter with the paradoxical feelings of being both abandoned and the abandoner. Adding to this crazy-making emotional set-up was the overly close relationship he had with his mother. Not only did she look to him for the tenderness and intimacy missing in her marriage, she also gave him sexual attention that repulsed, confused and stimulated him all at once.

At this point, the pain of the cumulative trauma became too much for Giermo to bear. The self-recrimination and shame he felt, his grief over the loss of his father as an adolescent boy, all piled up inside of him and had nowhere to go—that is, until he found drugs. Drugs and alcohol offered him a way out, a chemical solution to psychological and emotional pain. While they temporarily alleviated his inner turmoil, they completely interrupted his process of grieving. He never moved from stage two to stage three in Bowlby's grief dynamic because when his pain, anger and despair began to hurt, he medicated them with drugs and alcohol as a way of numbing these feelings. Consequently he wasn't motivated to work through his trauma. He remained, in a sense, stuck in yearning and searching, seeking to replace rather than feel his loss.

As an adult, Giermo had a series of relationships that all ended up with him feeling in some way abandoned. The male side of him rose up to fill in the gap left by his father, and he became a sort of magical husband for his mother in that child-like way of attempting to rebalance the family. Later, he kept choosing people who wanted him to "take care" of them, thus repeating the pattern of relating that had started with his parents. The more he feared he might be abandoned, the more attentive and solicitous he became. He alternated with women between feeling deep love, rage, hate and then a sort of cold indifference—the pattern of intense, emotional need and withdrawal so common in the trauma survivor. One of his mother's constant threats after the father left was that she was "just going to kill herself." Giermo finally connected his old hurt with the way he formed relationships in the present when he found himself visiting his fiancée, Rikki, in a psychiatric ward after her suicide attempt. She, like the mother, often threatened this, but it wasn't until the stark reality lay before him that he realized how he was living out old trauma in current life, unconsciously propelling himself toward the situations that he most deeply feared, in an attempt to somehow master, solve or get beyond them. His work was the work of stage three of the grief process, to feel the anger, disruption and despair surrounding his earlier losses and traumas so that he could begin to connect blocks and obsessions in present-day relating with the pain he carried from the past. Along with this came some of the maturational tasks that he had avoided through his years of addiction, such as committing himself to some life's work and taking the steps to make it real. Drugs and alcohol had effectively allowed him to postpone necessary, formative growth because they kept him sedated rather than grappling and struggling with the issues that encourage maturation.

How Unresolved Grief Affects Our Bodies

Traumatic experiences early in life can change the way we respond to stress later in life. As we discussed in the first chapter, the natural human response to trauma is (1) fight, (2) flight or (3) freeze. Any one of these responses precludes the full processing of emotional pain. The function of these responses is to ensure survival, to allow us to protect ourselves from immediate danger. They work for the moment, allowing us to continue to function, but eventually we need to feel and process these feelings that we put "on hold." If we do not feel them, they do not disappear—the "unfelt known" will seek relief. The feelings that were put on hold can cause psychological and physical problems throughout life.

Lawrence Brass, M.D., associate professor of neurology at Yale Medical School, recently completed studies that discovered severe stress is one of the most significant risk factors for stroke—even more so than high blood pressure—and this holds true as long as 50 years after the initial trauma. Brass studied 556 veterans of World War II. He found that the rate of stroke among those veterans who were prisoners of war was eight times higher than the stroke rate of soldiers who had not been captured. Brass was confused by the findings because the stress hormones that cause heart disease and stroke are elevated for only a few hours after a stressful event. "I began to realize we would have to take our understanding of stress further when I began to see that in some people stress can cause disease years after the initial event." He concluded, "The stress of being a POW was so severe it changed the way these folks responded to stress in the future—it sensitized them."

For the veterans who had been POWs, their neurochemical system was kicked off-kilter. Instead of churning out the normal amount of hormones in a stressful event, their system was dysregulated and, at the slightest provocation, either pumped out too much of some needed chemicals or not enough of others. "Years of this kind of hormonal assault may have weakened their cardiovascular system and led to the strokes" (Carpi, 1996).

Flashbacks and Overreactions

This example illuminates what can happen to the body as a result of trauma. Emotionally painful experiences get somatized, stored in the very tissue of the body. They lead not only to psychological pain but pain held on the cellular body level as well, referred to as "cellular memory." For those traumatized early in life, relationships in adulthood can become minefields triggering emotional explosions. Survivors of trauma actually react to the stresses of relationships *as if* they were reexperiencing the original situation all over again. They are physiologically and psychologically wired for overreaction. When this overreaction occurs, it feels threatening and confusing, leading the survivor to unconsciously revert to the emotional defenses that they used to cope with their early trauma. The memory may return in a sudden flash that comes and goes in the blink of an eye or an overreaction can get triggered then spill out into the relationship dynamic.

In his love relationships with women, Giermo tends to split. He alternated between seeing Rikki as all good or all bad. Idealization had been a defense that he used as a child in order to hide from himself the fear he had of his father's rage and his mother's overly sensualized interest in him. Because he felt fundamentally uncomfortable and at risk, idealizing served to keep his fears of the frightening sides of his parents at bay. It was just too much for him to integrate a father who beat him or a mother who was inappropriately interested in him into his image of and need for the parent he wished to have. Idealizing, however, was only a temporary solution at best and kept him from facing his true fears, vulnerability and helplessness. Consequently, when Rikki behaved in a way that triggered his old ghosts from childhood, he turned; the idealization gave way to its opposed feeling and she became all bad, the living representation of all he feared lurked beneath the surface of his parents.

All children have both loving and aggressive feelings toward their parents. These diverging feelings get integrated within children over time as they learn that their moments of hate do not end or ruin the relationship. In Giermo's case, there was little safety to feel either his anger toward his father or his wish for physical intimacy toward his mother because the parents had poor boundaries themselves in these areas. Expressing these feelings could have led to beatings or sexual intrusion, which felt all too real and dangerous to Giermo. Consequently, until therapy, he was not able to integrate both the good and bad sides of his parents and mature into seeing them as human beings. Later, that lack of integration evidenced itself in his own love relationships. Rikki changed in his mind from being the ideal mate with whom he could have the life he had always dreamed of to a woman who could potentially destroy him. Because he developed a high intensity/withdrawal inner world from living with trauma, he repeats that pattern in intimacy and tends to choose people with a similar set-up. If the relationship isn't intense, he has trouble staying connected. It feels dull to him, he feels unseen. Giermo fused love and pain at an early age and lived that out in relationships in adulthood.

A look, phrase or attitude from Rikki could be interpreted by Giermo through the lens of his early childhood experiences. His nervous system would unconsciously get triggered and his palms might sweat; he would feel anxious, rageful, even short of breath. Then he would act toward her as if she were the sole cause of his current pain. A seemingly minor incident could trigger a set of responses that had been hard-wired from childhood. As is often the case, Rikki had a similar emotional set-up. Consequently, the conflicts they entered into tended to escalate so quickly that resolution was difficult, if not impossible, until they did the painful, therapeutic work of unearthing the original wounds that were getting triggered by their current relationship. Once they began to identify their overreactions and link them to their original wounds, they were able to see more clearly how their past influenced their present, making it feel unmanageable. Separating their pasts from their present was key in helping them understand how their relationship conflicts became overwhelming and confusing.

How Words and Meaning
Get Fused Together

An example of how this reactiveness gets biologically set up is illustrated by experiments on how information is taken in by the brain. In one of Bowlby's research projects, subjects were given a small shock while particular word combinations were spoken to them. In response, subjects were conditioned to fear the shock and to associate it with those particular word combinations; Bowlby tracked this by measuring the subject's change in the (GSR) or their measure of sweating. This is how a psychological pattern of associating emotional pain with particular words, phrases, looks or gestures gets set up. Essentially he trained his subjects, by shocking them, to respond with fear when they heard certain words. Furthermore, when subjects were presented with homonyms or synonyms for those words, the change in the GSR also occurred. Thus, words that even approximate the meaning of those heard during highly stressful moments become loaded. This illustrates how words heard during a traumatic situation take on fearful or upsetting meaning that becomes established and hard-wired into the brain. The meaning of the words gets fused or associated with the fear and anxiety of the traumatic moment. Then, as victims go through the rest of their lives, they associate that web of meanings with those particular words, even when there is no danger or threat intended. This sets the stage for countless misinterpretations in subsequent relationships. The same phenomenon extends to associating meaning with particular actions, expressions or attitudes. The meaning that was established in a stressful "shocking" moment becomes part of the brain's storehouse of information that gets recalled when the person encounters those words, actions, expressions or attitudes again at another time in life.

This describes how an unconscious pattern gets set up. The fact that the meaning attached to the word is largely unconscious is a significant part of the problem, as a person has a strong reaction but doesn't understand its origins fully. This is why the first stage in healing is to let the emotional wound become conscious; however, it is just this sort of painful reaction that we often resist or defend against knowing. Simply allowing it to be known is more than a first step toward altering it.

Understanding this pattern seems to help people manage it more successfully. If you are aware that you may be biologically as well as emotionally set up for this type of overreaction, you are able to be compassionate rather than punitive with yourself. You aren't "crazy" after all. What you need from yourself at these times of overreaction are patience and understanding, not judgment and self-recrimination. Judgment and self-recrimination only keep the pattern in place because feelings of vulnerability and fear are never allowed to emerge past the defenses.

It is a thin membrane at best that divides the physical from the mental. They are interrelated, interdependent systems that operate most effectively when they operate in harmony. What we do with our bodies, how we eat, exercise and rest will affect our minds, and the way that we think and feel will affect our bodies.

How the Brain Takes In Information

It is no surprise, given the emotional legacy that trauma survivors live with, that they become hypervigilant, always scanning their environment or their relationships for signs of a problem. The way that hypervigilance gets set up becomes clearer when we understand the way in which the brain learns or processes the information that it constantly takes in from the outside.

Information taken in by the brain, according to Bowlby, can undergo one of several selection processes: (1) It can be completely excluded without leaving a trace—that is, the brain will not take it in at all; (2) it can be retained long enough outside of consciousness in a sort of buffer storage to influence judgment, autonomic responses and mood; or (3) it can reach a stage of advanced processing associated with conscious thought and intelligent cognitive functioning, and in doing so influence all levels of thinking, thereby becoming eligible for long-term storage.

This description of the subtle selection process the brain goes through opens the door to understanding how a person can avoid or dismiss information that the brain "forbids knowing." That is to say, the brain is influenced in what it accepts or rejects by what it already knows or is willing to accept. With split-second timing it scans the inflow of information, analyzing and evaluating it in terms of knowledge already stored or filed on the subject, and then sends commands to an encoder as to what should be kept and what should be rejected or discarded. Thus, someone who has a pattern of repression or denial can maintain this pattern with little conscious awareness, as perception happens so quickly and is largely subliminal.

As Bowlby explains:

> Not only does all this preliminary scanning and storing take place outside awareness but information rejected at this stage is likely to be permanently lost, although as in the experimental study, this may not always be so. This is the stage at which perceptual defense or vigilance is postulated to take place. The upshot is that, provided these representational models and programs are well adapted, the fact that they are drawn on automatically and without awareness is a great advantage. When, however, they are not well adapted, for whatever reason, the disadvantages of the arrangement become serious. As anyone who has developed a bad style in some physical skill knows well, to review the cognitive and action components of a system that has

long been automated and to change it is arduous and often frus-
trating; moreover, it is not always very successful. Hence, some
of the difficulties encountered during psychotherapy. You can't
teach an old dog new tricks. This, however, is not the only problem nor the greatest, for the task of changing an over learned
program of action and/or of appraisal is enormously exacerbated
when roles long implemented by the valuative system forbid its
being reviewed. (Bowlby, 1980, p. 55, 56)

Trauma survivors who have adopted and repeated maladaptive or dysfunctional relationship styles that they learned as children find it difficult to retrain those styles in adulthood. To add
to the problem, retraining those styles requires that they first be
reviewed—which, in the case of survivors of trauma, requires
that the survivor reexperience the emotional pain, hurt, helplessness, rage and vulnerability associated with the original hurt
before "retraining" the behavior. As Daniel Akron describes this
in his research on how the brain learns,

> Individual brain cells, after repeated exposure to similar
> events, begin to react in the same fashion each time: In other
> words, they learn. The human brain then starts to categorize
> and [to] group images, and then we use these complex sets to
> make abstractions. This process, created and reinforced in child-
> hood, creates memories, which rarely go away. They may be
> hidden from the conscious mind, but they remain locked in the
> brain, waiting for a trigger to bring them to the surface.
> (Dawson, 1993)

When we speak of psychological trauma, we are looking at a
broad range of wounds from neglect, divorce or separation to
overt abuse.

Perceptual defense, along with what the brain has learned, are
core features determining whether or not a person is emotionally
set up and capable of healthy mourning later in life. Because in the

process of mourning it is necessary to accept the full reality of a situation, people who are prone to splitting off painful or unwanted thoughts and feelings and relegating them to a part of the brain that is excluded from conscious awareness are not able to sit with the full reality of a painful circumstance and process their thoughts and feelings. People who are prone to defensive exclusion are handicapped in their relationships with others and the world, and are more likely to suffer breakdowns in functioning for periods lasting weeks, months or years because they are impaired in dealing effectively with problems that arise in their lives.

Experiential Triggers:
It's Happening All Over Again

This phenomenon clearly underscores how a coping pattern gets set up. Once set up, it waits for experiential triggers that set it into motion. Hence, words, life events, something as seemingly mild as a threatening look or attitude can trigger a coping pattern that has little to do with the actual event. In looking at Marla's story, we see how this phenomenon gets lived out in day-to-day life.

Marla was hypervigilant around the subject of criticism. The daughter of Russian immigrants, the pressure on her to succeed in America, coupled with the lack of parental support in assisting her to feel comfortable and at home in her world, made the heavy expectations from her father feel like an impossible standard—even though she tried desperately to meet them. Marla was a very bright child and was capable of being a successful student, but she lacked the social comfort to make friends easily. All of her energy went toward pleasing her teacher and little or none toward socializing, a pattern set up at home. The only photographs that she has of herself as a child are ones in which she was playing a specific role: Marla as a Girl Scout, a graduate, a swimmer and so on. She has no photographs of herself or her family just being together enjoying each other's company, nor did they take family vacations. The high standards set by her father were without the relief of other types of playful activity. These standards and the way she felt separated her in her own mind from the other children; served on the one hand to motivate her into high achievement and on the other to block her ability to enjoy or feel comfortable with it. Not surprisingly, she carried her fear of criticism and authority into her workplace.

Recently, Marla came to our therapy group very worried over an upcoming yearly evaluation. Because of her experience as a child she emotionally defended against acknowledging her fear of criticism. After all, if her father was the head of the household, he must be right. In her mind (as a child), he had no problem with being overly critical; it was she who was unworthy of praise, she who was underperforming. When confronted with her boss's yearly review, she kept running over her performance in her mind, searching for areas in which she might be called to task. Her anxiety level rose daily as she anticipated what she may have done "wrong." She had a less successful year than the previous one, and in Marla's ideal of how she should perform, there was little room for mistakes. The fact that the entire stock market had taken a plunge was no excuse. How she performed felt like who she was, so criticism of her performance felt like criticism of her very self. There was little space between the two and no room for error.

In Marla's case, her boss's impending critique returned her to feeling like a little girl who wasn't getting it right for Daddy—a little girl who wasn't good enough and didn't know what to do to correct it. Daddy had not been helpful in showing Marla how to meet his expectations, nor in letting her know that she was his beloved little girl no matter what her performance. Further, although Marla's mother acknowledged that her husband was overly critical and demanding of his children, her response to the equally unrealistic demands he placed on her was to placate him rather than challenge his self-serving standard. Rather, Marla's mother took the problem onto herself and catered to her husband instead of challenging his burdensome standards. Consequently, Marla learned through modeling to accept outside criticism, however unrealistic, as accurate, and defended against knowing that a man might have his own complicated problems with low self-esteem that come out in the form of hypercriticism. In addition, she was actually being called upon as a child to enhance the self-esteem of her whole family by succeeding in a world in which they felt their own options were limited.

The upshot of all this was that Marla's insides didn't match her outsides, and while on the outside she was a very successful fund manager, on the inside she felt like a failure. When she shared these vulnerable feelings in group, she was able to understand why her boss's upcoming yearly review felt like a walk to the gallows. When she was able to make these connections and realize the problem was not just with her, she became less fearful and anxious about the event; and when it actually took place, she realized that she was indeed her own harshest critic, as her employer's review of her was much more favorable than her own self-review. The pain she experienced as a child needed to be felt so she could separate her issues from her father's. The review process then turned out to be healing rather than retraumatizing, as she placed her fears in a realistic context.

The Coping Pattern

The wounds suffered in childhood are interpreted through the mind of a child, with the reasoning available to him or her at a particular developmental stage. What happens during youth gets stored *as it was interpreted at that time.*

Each person has a pattern of dealing with grief around loss that is unique to him or her. It grows out of a combination of factors such as modeling early-life losses and experiences around moments of significant life transition. Modeling the ways in which loss or pain was dealt with by those who raised us becomes an example that we draw on unconsciously throughout life. A second factor is how early-life losses and problems were experienced and processed and what meaning we made out of them. If traumatized feelings were worked through and resolved, we tend to learn from them; if they were not, the unresolved feelings remain within the unconscious, waiting to be triggered by current life issues. Hence intense, confusing emotions and distorted meanings become part of our reactive coping pattern in dealing with later loss. A third factor is significant life transition (see pages 79-84). How these sensitive stages were experienced affects our sense of safety around loss.

People make meaning out of loss and trauma as a way of coping or explaining it to themselves. Children make meaning out of divorce, adults make meaning out of life losses, and this meaning becomes part of a script that gets acted out throughout life.

> Grieving children make sense of overwhelming experience with the tools of the developmental moment weaving together a web of associations and meanings that presents their best capacity at the time to face and master the event. Aspects of experience that are overwhelming are repressed or disassociated from gathering with them aspects of the child's development that were intertwined with the stressful event and with the child's attempt to cope. The trade-off seems worthwhile at the time of the original event, for the child gains stability and reduces conflict with important others. However, this is accomplished at the expense of full development of the child's capacities which, denies the child the possibility of optimal functioning. (Shapiro, 1994, p. 62)

This interpretation becomes part of the script. Part of reframing and creating a new pattern is examining these interpretations and bringing them up to speed so that the old tape—though it may emerge—can be interrupted and retrained.

The Apple Doesn't Fall Far from the Tree: How Does a Coping Style Get Acted Out Later in Life?

Much of the way that we behave is learned, and the family in which we grow up offers our core curriculum. In the classroom of the family, we learn our most profound lessons on how to conduct relationships. We enter this classroom as babies, totally dependent upon our parents for our survival. We look to these people to sustain our lives, and we are biologically set up to meet our developmental needs through these kinship relationships. We know instinctively to whom we belong—my mommy, my daddy, my sister or brother. The cry of the infant calls the parent to action with greater speed than any army bugle could command. Nature has set up the family as the survival unit of society. What we learn in this unit, we learn through a hunger for nurturance, a hunger to know who we are, a hunger to live. It is no wonder, then, that the way these people upon whom we are so totally dependent see us comes to paint the picture of how we see ourselves. Nothing means more to us as children than the love and acceptance of this family in which we are growing into the person we will one day become. The way in which we are touched becomes the way in which we touch, the way in which we are spoken to becomes the way we speak to others, and the way in which we are seen and understood becomes the way in which we see and understand ourselves and our world. Then we go out onto the stage of life and we practice what we have learned. The good and productive lessons we learned help us to re-create sustaining and nurturing relationships in our adult lives. The painful or dysfunctional patterns we have learned get in the way of the health of those relationships. Children who come from divorced homes, according to research done by Judith Wallerstein, grow up with deep and lasting wounds that affect their productivity as adults and cause them to fear that they cannot sustain long-term relationships of their own. Children who grow up with addiction often exhibit the cluster of characteristics known as Post-Traumatic Stress Disorder referred to in the charts preceding each chapter of this book.

We reveal our life story through our repetitions. A compulsion to repeat a particular behavior or to bring an experience toward us over and over again, even if it is not productive, can be seen as an unconscious attempt to understand or solve an issue from the past around which there is unresolved grief and trauma. Examining needs and motivations that drive us toward bumping up against the same old wall can tell us much about *how* we experienced our early losses and the meanings we assigned to them. Repetitions can be seen as unconscious cries for help and provide important information about the self.

The Elephant in the Living Room: Family Coping Styles

The manner in which we cope with painful situations may have been learned in the families in which we grew up. The following are some dysfunctional ways in which families may cope with loss that lead to problems for family members.

Emotional avoidance is one pathological coping style in which a loss or trauma is not spoken of, whether it be loss of a person to addiction, psychological illness, divorce or separation. This is the "elephant in the living room" syndrome. The problem looms large in the emotional container of the family, but no one is able to speak of it. Consequently, family members find themselves walking on eggshells, saying everything but that which weighs so heavily upon their hearts. Children in these situations are at risk for being the symptom-bearers or scapegoats of unspoken family pain and tension.

The *scapegoat* is the member of the family on whom the family pain gets projected. Families who are in denial of their pain often identify one member to become preoccupied and worried about. This scapegoating diverts the families' attention from the real problem by giving it another focus. Needless to say, it solves nothing, confuses the issues even more and creates a highly problematic and toxic identity for the scapegoat.

Another pathological coping style is *family cutoff*—to cut off ties with or segregate a family member who is not maintaining the status quo, gathering some family members together and cutting off another. Problems get projected or transferred onto the children as a way of taking the focus off the tension and anxiety that the parents do not wish to look at in their own relationship; thus a child can become a scapegoat for family pain.

Let me illustrate how a complex developed in childhood affected Connie's trust and comfort in her marriage to Bill. Connie's childhood trauma sat inside her, in adulthood, as an unhealed wound, and whenever it got triggered it distorted and disturbed her adult relating pattern.

Connie experiences conflict frequently when she feels she is missing something or changing plans. By the time she was 14, the family she had known had ended and the five years preceding that were a nightmare of alcoholism, sexual invasion, hurt and fear. One of the only things she had to hang on to from her family was a sense of loss—somehow feeling a sense of loss made her feel less alone, as if there was still something left of her family with which to connect. After 10-plus happy years with her husband and children, she feels this should be behind her, but she still feels the effects of that early trauma when she is confronted with making a decision. She has unrealistic fears about making the wrong choice. She has trouble balancing options. If, for example, she decides to take a vacation away from her children, she spends much of it worrying about them, wishing she were home. Then when she arrives home, she regrets the place she left. She worries that she should be living near her family of origin, though she is quite happily situated where she is and has a full and interesting life. She is prone to guilt and regret when something goes badly for her children or husband and tortures herself by going over each and every decision and action taken that might have contributed to a problem. Connie has abandonment issues that manifest in a variety of forms. Even deciding what to eat from a menu can feel a bit baffling on occasion. Her constant worry that her family might end can be traced to a childhood trauma with her family of origin.

Connie didn't know her father was leaving or that her mother had served divorce papers to him. One day she came home from school and he was gone. No one prepared her, no one helped her through the pain of his absence; they forgot. They were so absorbed in their own pain that they forgot to tell her what was going on. In sessions, Connie talks about how she used to look at her husband Bill's clothes in the closet as a way of telling herself that he would surely come back at the end of the day. As she looks back on that now, she wonders why it didn't occur to her that he would come back to her. She had learned an awful lesson as a teenager—that someone could forget to tell her they were leaving—and the trauma of that made her see relationships in black-and-white terms: She and Bill were either super-connected or lost to each other. Anything was better than the latter. She would rather be engaged in a low-level fight for days and feel connected than feel her fear of abandonment. She had trouble allowing herself to count on the good times lasting.

Now that she understands this, she can translate it into an awareness of not taking Bill for granted, but before she processed the pain she was held to a cycle of reenactment— intense closeness, pushing one another away, then passionate reconnection, anything to keep from falling into an abyss of nothingness—anything but being forgotten.

Connie was caught in a pattern of anxiety and worry that manifested itself through a feeling that she was missing out on something, that if she made a wrong decision, she would experience some terrible loss. When she could uncover her memories over her father's departure and how it was handled at the time, then connect her current anxiety over fear of Bill's disappearing with that of her father's, she could come to some inner peace around the whole issue. In a sense, Connie's loyalty to her father expressed itself in her constant preoccupation with his loss both in her family of origin and with Bill. Because her family did not openly mourn or discuss her missing father, Connie kept his presence alive within the family by worrying about him, memorializing his absence by her constant preoccupation. Because the entire family was also unconsciously preoccupied with the loss of the father, Connie's constant concern "held" or "contained" the family's unspoken pain. Until the family could speak about the father openly and his loss within the family system, they could not heal and reorganize the family structure.

When grief over the loss of a family member is not openly spoken, the family is not able to integrate the loss. Rather, the loss goes underground, so to speak, often resulting in family members acting out pain in behavioral problems. Also, the pain needs to be shared so that family members do not become estranged from each other. Loss can become a bonding experience if it is shared openly or an alienating one if it is not.

Working with the Pattern: Creating Change

Psychological health and physical health are greatly enhanced, according to Henry Dreher, author of *The Immune Power Personality,* by our ability to *attend, connect* and *express* our feelings and thoughts. First we *attend,* we tune in to our inner states: What is going on within me that I need to pay attention to? Once we have allowed the feelings and thoughts to be felt, we are in a position to *connect*—to link the feeling state with the appropriate situation, whether it be an inner situation that we carry from our past or an outer one that is occurring in life. When we come closer to understanding what is going on with us, we can then *express* or find appropriate ways of sharing what we are experiencing. This simple process of attending, connecting and expressing has curative, if not merely health-sustaining, features. It elevates monocytes and lymphocytes in the blood, which translates into a stronger immune system. The same benefits are experienced through thinking thoughts that are uplifting. In studies using two control groups, one group was given movies to watch on Mother Teresa, while the other was given movies on Nazi war acts. The group watching Mother Teresa showed elevations in disease-fighting antibodies. The group watching the Nazi war acts had no change or even depressed immune systems. Within an hour all counts returned to normal—however, when each group was asked to consciously think about and visualize these movies throughout a day, the Mother Teresa group maintained benefits while the Nazi war act group maintained lower antibody levels (Dreher, 1995).

The Benefits of a Positive Attitude

One can surely extrapolate these results into other areas. An uplifted psychological and spiritual attitude actually promotes and creates good health, while negative thinking or exposure to fighting and violence undermines it. Understanding the self, being aware of feeling states, sharing feelings with others that break isolation and enhance support have been proven through research to affect health. The mind cannot be separated from the body. Repressed grief depresses the immune system. Repression undermines health. A grief process is as important to physical health as it is to psychological health.

If we deny what we are feeling, we cannot attend, connect and express because we have lost access to our internal world. Denying our real feelings gives them a power within the self-system that actually has physical as well as psychological impact. Then, depending on our personality, we may try to numb them, medicate them or act them out in self-destructive ways. A process of grief allows us to take care of personal business so that it does not become an emotional infection. It allows us to clean a wound and let it heal. Understanding the natural architecture of the stages of grieving provides a map to follow in healing trauma or loss. The combination of opening to the grief process and finding a safe place in which to share feelings is a model that imitates community and ritual. Ritual in many religions marks the stages of grieving, and the community provides the safe container in which to come in touch with and express feelings. This basic model can be re-created or returned to in modern society through friends, family, support groups, social institutions, churches, temples and synagogues.

A study by public health researchers Lisa F. Berkman, Ph.D., of Yale University and F. Leonard Syne, Ph.D., of the University of California, Berkeley, took nine years to complete and involved nearly 7,000 residents of Alameda County, California. The objective was to systematically assess four specific sources of social support—marriage, contacts with close friends and relatives, church membership and informal group associations. The results confirmed that "people with social ties, no matter what the source, lived longer than isolated people. This held true regardless of cigarette smoking, alcohol consumption, obesity, sleeping, eating habits and medical care" (Padus, 1992, p. 17).

Repression, isolation and negative thinking frequently work their way into people's patterns of dealing with loss. Turning these around through solutions such as therapy, support groups, engineered family rituals and reunions and spiritual life are central to changing this pattern. Because our society has become so mobile and life spans have lengthened, people face significant losses more frequently due to moving away from extended families and living through more stages of life. Each new stage of life has both gains and losses woven into it.

> . . . for centuries the very young have outnumbered the very old. . . . In 1950 there were nearly two under five, for every person over 60. But by 2025 grandparents will outnumber babies two to one. Two well established trends are causing this dramatic shift in population structure—fewer babies and longer lives. Life expectancy is predicted to rise from 47 to 70 years of age, turning the population pyramid upside down (United Nations, 1982).

At the turn of this century, the average male had a life expectancy of 35 to 47 years of age; by the year 2025, about a century later, that will have risen, adding almost three decades of life to each man. The average American will move 14 to 17 times in the course of his or her life. Life loss is part of a mobile, longer-lived society. Learning how to cope with life loss in an effective way is a growing need in this century, so that in our unresolved pain at losing we do not create more alienation than necessary. Isn't it possible that some of our preoccupation with dysfunctional families is an attempt to heal families that have not learned to function well in a mobile society—to accept and incorporate change and distance without turning it into loss and alienation? Dysfunctional patterns may come from inexperience in dealing with unknown lifestyles as well as from pathology. Examining personal loss patterns offers, paradoxically, a way of keeping more, in a sense, by becoming a "good loser"—that is, learning how to accommodate life losses without overreacting to them and losing more than necessary.

Tears, the Natural Healer

According to William H. Frey II, a Minnesota biochemist, "the reason people feel better after crying is that they may be removing, in their tears, chemicals that build up during emotional stress. Thus when people use the expression 'to cry it out,' we are suggesting that this may literally be true" (Suplee, 1987). All other excretory functions, Frey observes, serve to remove noxious and/or waste substances from the body. Why not tears?

According to recent laboratory analysis, the tears that are shed in grief have a different chemical composition from other kinds of tears. Emotional crying is apparently not a learned behavior, since children who are born deaf and blind still weep. "And it is triggered by a still-unknown neurologic process: If the ophthalmic branch of the fifth facial nerve is severed, reflex or irritant weeping is inhibited; emotional tears are, however, unaffected" (Suplee, 1987).

Tears, then, are one of the body's ways of releasing toxic chemicals and restoring equilibrium. In an article in *Ms.* magazine, it was reported that many women intuitively know the healing in crying. "Many women are quite methodical about having a 'good cry,' actually choosing a time, place and immediate stimulus to tears. It could be an hour in the bathtub or a date with yourself to watch *Wuthering Heights* or the late show." Crying, then, is a helpful part of the process of mourning, both physically and psychologically (Suplee, 1987).

Pain Turned Inward: Laura's Story

Loss and trauma can be turned against the self in personally destructive ways. Laura's story represents a deep descent through the corridors of psychic pain. Her way of trying to control her inner experience of fragmentation and emotional pain was to self-mutilate—that is, to injure herself. Though this is tragic and somewhat horrifying, it is more common than one might think. As Laura spoke of this in group, she assumed a still, almost rigid pose and fixed her gaze downward, as if bracing herself while she went within to observe the contents of her mind.

There were hardly any spaces for breathing in Laura's delivery of her story. As she explained her life—in between words and phrases—she withdrew her breath over and over in quiet gasps. She had recently been suicidal. Her arms were marked and scarred from where she had used a needle not only to inject drugs but to self-mutilate. She had no memory whatsoever of the long periods of time she spent injuring herself. She remembered only a vague sense of emotional pain and its momentary relief. Her cutting represented a dip into psychosis, into a world detached from reality. Self-injury was for her a way of temporarily releasing deeply held pain, intense emotional hurt and anger that had nowhere to go. Some people yell or hurt others, some kick and scream, some, like Laura, hurt themselves. Laura wore long sleeves. The shame she felt and the need to explain to others why her arms were scarred were too much to bear.

Where would she begin? She could hardly explain it to herself. Unraveling the mystery of her own life, of her story, of the trauma and grief that led her to suicide attempts and self-injury was out of her conscious reach. Laura, like so many like her, felt that she was the problem. She recalls as a child waiting in frozen anticipation for her father to return home from work, at which time her mother would feed him all of Laura's missteps of the day. The mother would regularly prepare a list of Laura's indiscretions, which resulted in the father's beating her with the buckle end of his belt. She recalls seeing blood on the walls. She remembers it as if she were watching from a few feet away and talks about it as if it happened to someone else. Only now and then does she allow herself to enter into the memory. But to fully accept it she would also have to feel the hate, confusion and betrayal that she carries inside of herself. What was wrong with her that her mother hated her so? She tried to be more of what her mother liked, but no matter what she improved, it was never enough. And why did her adored father turn against her in this way? She reported to the group that she was the apple of her father's eye and that her mother, contrary to what we might think, was a wonderful woman. It was Laura who was the problem, she said, and she wished that therapy might help her to discover what was wrong with herself so that she might set about changing it. Maybe then she could finally deserve the love and acceptance she so sorely wished for—and maybe then she could begin to accept herself.

Therapy with Laura was going to take time. Dismantling her idealizations of her parents needed to be careful work. As a child, she carefully constructed the parents that she wished she had in order to make herself feel safe in the custody of the parents she actually did have. Had she let herself know that it was her parents who had the problem, she would have felt too unsafe in their presence. And where could she go as an eight-year-old girl? There was only one other alternative left—she must be bad. This, at least, gave her hope and some sense of control. If she were bad then maybe she could get better; then her parents would be sure to like her and she could finally get the love and nurturing she needed. The deep despair that Laura carried but repressed, tucked away into a corner of her mind, built up slowly over time. The pain of the situation she lived in was too much for her, so she used the defenses available to her at that time, childhood defenses, in order to make her situation tolerable. She concocted a life that she could live with and parents who were safe, transforming the sides of them that frightened her into a picture of her parents that she found less threatening. She wove a fantasy to replace the reality.

Laura also learned to dissociate from pain, to psychically leave her body and watch the beating from a safe distance. This same dissociation was lived out with her self-injuring—the blood on the walls was as far away and strange to her as the blood on her arms. In order to heal her tendency to self-hurt, she needed to go back to her father's beatings and her mother's betrayal, to feel the pain of that so she could feel the pain she was causing herself. More than physical, this was an emotional pain, the pain of betrayal, the disillusionment of seeing the highly conflicting sides of her father and mother and integrating those rather than splitting them off. In splitting them off, she only allowed herself to see their good side—the parents who adored her and would never wish her harm—while she relegated the parents who hurt her to her unconscious. While the "bad" father remained hidden, he came out in her own self-abuse and the abusive men she was intimate with. She did to herself what her father did to her, perpetuating the myth that she was bad and needed punishing, keeping the family system intact inside of her. In disassembling this and allowing the underbelly of the abusive family system to become conscious, much deep feeling gets released. Luckily in psychodrama, we can provide a place for it to go. Misery and pain seek an object at which to direct the feelings in the healing process so that the hatred that has been turned against the self can be redirected. An empty chair representing either a person or an aspect of self or a surrogate role-player can allow for this release of strong emotion. Laura chose other group members to play her mother and father in a variety of vignettes over a period of several years. Each piece of work revealed another piece of the puzzle.

For Laura, all this was not only a matter of exhaling anger and resentment but of coming in touch with the deep hurt and shame she carried in relationship to these dynamics. Then she needed to let in support and acceptance, creating a new baseline of learning, opening a new "storage file" within her for caring experience. She had always seen herself as at fault, as deserving of punishment, and so she had internalized these models and treated herself as she was treated. The beaten child became the beater, and her beatings took the form of self-injury. She slowly started to reveal her fear of ever having children because she was afraid she might hurt them. Instead, she remained single after her divorce from a co-addict and hurt herself—almost to death.

Undoing this outer dynamic turned inward was a tender process, allowing the idealization to crumble slowly and be replaced by a more realistic understanding of who her parents were as people. Then she constructed corrective experiences so that she could learn how healthy intimacy feels. Part of the work was to go back a generation and do work with her mother and her grandmother.

One of the most powerful psychodramas I did with Laura revealed a grandmother who had disowned her daughter (Laura's mother), refusing to speak with her because she disapproved of her marriage, and who had formed an unholy alliance with the son (Laura's uncle), colluding against the daughter. Laura set up a scene she remembered in which her mother stood in the street looking up longingly at the lights burning in the grandmother's apartment. I asked Laura to reverse roles with her mother and to "stand in her shoes" for a moment. From this vantage point, Laura, as her mother, found herself wondering what was wrong with her that had caused her to be cast out by her own mother (the grandmother). The sadness and hurt that

Laura felt in the role of her mother were eye-opening. When she came back to her own role she could not help but see her mother differently, seeing not only a tyrannical mother but a wounded daughter rejected and hated by her mother, with no understanding of why. Laura's mother had simply passed on her pain. The abuse she received *as* a daughter she acted out *on* her daughter; so goes the gruesome dance of generational dysfunction.

Embracing Our Inner World

All too often we think of grief as a collapsing into rather than a surrender. But standing by—holding the inner experience, honoring the depth of pain and loss—is an expression of love and respect for self and others. The adult self allows the child self to cry fully, to be hurt and angry, to feel despair, confusion and disorientation while the inner adult witnesses. The gifts that this provides are obvious. We get to know ourselves; we allow our vulnerable sides to live, breathe and feel; we integrate the pain of grief into the self-system rather than flash-freezing it, giving it psychic storage space but no voice or breath. In addition, as the adult self witnesses the volatile inner experience of the child self, that inner world is demystified. The adult observes and thinks, develops insights and heightens awareness about the inner child self and that child's emotional inner world. Only then is the adult self in a position to guide and sustain the child self—not crush or ignore but embrace and lead.

We think of the self as unidimensional, but in truth the inner world is complex and full of differing aspects that corelate in creating the whole. Someone needs to be in the driver's seat, to organize the whole, and that someone is the adult self. It is the relationship that the adult self has to the other aspects of self that fosters inner contentment. Our early relationships are carried through life in our inner world, though they are learned from our outer world. The position that the father took toward the son becomes internalized within the son as a part of the inner adult. The son learns how to "father" himself from the father he knew, then incorporates that learning into his own inner world, where he continues to father himself in a manner informed, in part, for better or worse, by the father who taught him. The same phenomenon occurs when the mother, siblings or other significant people are internalized. We learn much of how to treat ourselves by the way that we were treated. The good news is that these inner dynamics can be significantly altered at any point in life by creating new experiences that ameliorate the old ones.

How Emotional Shutdown Gets Carried into Adult Intimate Relationships

Experiencing powerful feelings in intimate love relationships can feel frightening to a person who has learned to shut feelings down in earlier intimate relationships. We learn how to be intimate very early in life and we carry that learning with us into partnership and family.

A trauma means that something has happened that is out of the ordinary and is difficult for the mind to integrate into its organizational model of what is normal. During an episode of acute stress or trauma, survival mechanisms encoded into the early or reptilian brain are engaged. The body is flooded with hormones that can make time and space feel as if they are slowing down or expanding. A situation takes on an air of unbelievability as if it weren't really happening. The more traumatic or out of the normal context of living an event is, the greater may be a person's urge to deny its impact—it feels too strange—without reference to other areas of life. It does not fit into life as we understand it. R. J. Lifton, in his studies of Hiroshima victims, described their numbness as "so powerful that it became a permanent part of their personalities."

While numbness is a primitive response to trauma, natural to our very being, denial might be seen, in part, as the intellect's attempt to explain that shutdown. "It doesn't hurt that much, it's not that bad, it's not such a big deal" are ways of minimizing a situation or diminishing its importance so that it feels less unmanageable. Denial can also be an attempt to rewrite a situation in an effort to make it seem less threatening. Often alcoholism and drug addiction are accompanied by significant denial. Because the changes within a person or a family usually happen slowly and over time, the problems caused to the addicted individual and those in the family system can be excused or rewritten as they occur. While the grief is denied and diverted, the deeper wound remains hidden and unattended to. Diverting grief provides temporary relief, but it does not heal it. Unless the wound is identified for what it is, the person or people carrying it will not be able to make meaningful connections between the pain over a loss and how that pain is being played out in their thinking, emotions and behavior in the world.

Warning Signs of Unresolved Grief and Its Effect on the Dynamics of Relating

Caretaking: In studies done by John Bowlby on primates and human mothers and infants, caretaking behavior emerged as one of the most immediate and pervasive responses to loss and separation. Perhaps it is the natural response to give the kind of attention that we feel is missing to another person as a way of feeling whole or of comforting the loss in our own self that motivates this behavior, or maybe it displaces the pain that we feel at losing comfort and care by immediately seeing someone else as being in need of it. Perhaps it is because comfort and care are, at their core, a mutual experience. Also, projection can play a role if the feeling that is missing within ourselves is then projected onto someone else, which is often less painful than owning it within the self.

In intimate relationships, caretaking complicates intimacy because the person doing the caretaking may really be responding to his or her own need for comfort, and the person receiving the caretaking is not necessarily in need of it. Owning the need for comfort, reassurance and safety, and articulating it to a partner is one of the ways of healing.

Extreme anger: When there is extreme anger to the exclusion of other symptoms, it is often an indication that someone has lost a person on whom he or she has been pathologically dependent, so that the person feels that his or her very survival is threatened by the loss of this person, who may be a symbolic link to childhood, the angry person's sense of well-being or self. "The entire bereavement experience is taken up with intense and furious rage; there is little yearning and pining and no sorrow—only protest. Although basic feelings may occur in the early stage of a complicated bereavement, they are accompanied by other grief responses, such as yearning or sadness, and eventually pass. In contrast, in this reaction, pattern anger persists, often becoming a destructive element in the mourner's life" (Rando, 1993, p. 66-77). In intimate relationships, if this is unresolved hostility, it may be taken out indirectly or through passive aggressive behavior on the partner (Rando, 1993).

Extreme guilt: Extreme guilt is another variation of distorted grief, tending to follow the loss of relationships that were intensely ambivalent and in which active fantasies about the death of the other were common. "The connection in the relationship is strong but negative in whole or in part. Whether in death or loss by separation, when the connection with a person has been highly ambivalent, the mourner feels guilty about their conflicting emotions for the person they lost and the loss can appear even as a wish fulfilled, so that the mourner feels a need to self punish for the destructive wish. Little direct anger is evident, although much hostility may be apparent." Some people who carry excessive guilt cannot bear the feeling and so project it onto others through blame, or deny its presence within themselves. Persistent guilt is also very preoccupying and can make the partner experiencing it somewhat emotionally unavailable because he or she is lost in his or her own preoccupations or patterns.

Depression: When someone is unnaturally preoccupied with guilt, "the need to self punish becomes strong and persistent" (Rando, 1993, p. 66-77). This need is often associated with severe depression evolving out of the loss. Anger, too, when turned inward onto the self, can lead to depression. In an intimate relationship, when one of the partners is depressed, that depressed partner can feel lost to the other person. This can greatly affect the emotional climate of the relationship. Another cause of depression can be unfelt sadness; sorrow over a loss that is not fully acknowledged and felt can deaden a person's emotional inner world and reduce spontaneity and interest in self, others and life in general.

Emotional numbness: Emotional numbness is a common symptom of unresolved grief and can last anywhere from minutes to hours to decades. It is characterized by a lack of emotional responsiveness and spontaneity. Emotional numbness inhibits a person's ability to respond to the subtle vicissitudes of any relationship. It is a defense against strong feelings, and because intimate relationships contain powerful emotions, the inability to feel or stay with them works against the partner's ability to remain present in an emotionally charged relationship climate. It works on subtler levels as well, decreasing a person's willingness to move in and out of aspects of the relationship that require staying present with strong feelings. In order to communicate feelings, it is necessary first to feel and describe them within the self and then find words to communicate that inner world to the other person. The partner of someone who is emotionally numb can feel frustrated, as if he or she has lost access to or is disconnected from the emotional world of the other person.

Self-mutilation: Bowlby discovered in his experiments with primates and mothers and infants that self-mutilation is a common result of loss and separation. It can take the form of picking, slapping the self, excessive rocking or head banging. These are only some of the forms. Others are cutting and self-injury. Though on the surface this is a symptom of unresolved grief that exclusively affects one person, it would follow that being in an intimate relationship with someone who is actively hurting himself or herself is doing pain to both members. It is this writer's feeling that there are subtler forms of self-injury that may take the form of driving the self to excess with no rest, self-destructive personal habits, or doing injury to the body through excessive exercise, starving or overfeeding it.

Necessary Losses: Natural Losses Over Stages of Life

Major life transitions and maturational losses can significantly impact how we learn to deal with loss. Separation and loss are an inevitable part of transition and change. How that separation is handled by all experiencing it shapes what loss comes to mean for each individual. The following are significant transitions—the meaning that children, adolescents and young adults make out of these points of transition is carried within their lifelong pattern of dealing with loss.

18 months: Prior to this age the parent/child relationship is one of co-relatedness; for children, it is hard to know where they leave off and their parents begin, so entwined are their inner worlds. At 18 months children begin to exhibit a drive toward more autonomy. The words "me," "my" and "no" become primary in their vocabulary. It is crucial at this stage that parents or caretakers remain readily available so that children can find them after short periods of separation to learn that it is safe to leave and safe to come back, that they will not lose their stability zone by leaving it—that they are assured a round-trip ticket both to and from their parents. In this way children learn to slowly incorporate into themselves the security experienced with the parents. They learn to take this feeling within them as they explore and expand the parameters of their world, then return and refuel at their parents' knee. The inevitable grief at the dawning of a sense of separateness from the parent may become loaded with anxiety and greatly exacerbated if children feel they are losing easy access. In that case, they may become anxious or depressed.

Adolescence: Adolescence is the onset of another significant period of parent/child separation. Children stand at the gap between childhood and adulthood, at once rejecting and yearning for both. In adolescents' bedrooms, you might find anything from teddy bears to condoms, symbols of their wide swing between two stages of life. They try on adult roles and regress to child ones in the blink of an eye. Adolescents desperately need parents to stand firm enough to withstand a mighty shove. They are moving away, and their journey feels both terrifying and thrilling to them. At the same time, they both mourn the loss of childhood and feel anticipatory grief at their fear around becoming an adult. How parents handle this stage will cut deep for the adolescent. Do the parents take the adolescent's wish to separate as a personal rejection of them? Do they create a container that can live with the widely vacillating roles that the adolescent lives out, or do they give the message that the adolescent separates at risk of losing parental love? If this is the case, separation can come to mean bone-chilling aloneness. If separation is tolerated and the parent does not withdraw love, nurturing and guidance, the adolescent will have a better chance at a sense of safety during self-exploration and can more easily carry the parent within himself or herself as a nurturing inner presence.

Young adulthood: This might be seen as a stage both of separation and rapprochement. Hopefully young adults have enough autonomy and secure sense of self to be able to return and reunite comfortably with parents. Separation is now serious business; they really are on their own, and while this is a liberation, it is also a deep loss of security. The comfort and support of a loving parent at this stage can be a tremendous source of security for the young adult. The relationship will need to alter in order to contain two adults, still parent and child but also friends, with room and respect for each individual's personhood. This is another stage where loss can be tremendously painful if, once the child is launched, so to speak, the launching pad is withdrawn. If home base disappears, young adults can feel they are floating in space alone, with little assistance in navigating the world in which they are just beginning to travel. The lesson young adults need to learn at each stage is that their wish to be their own person will not cost them the love and blessing of their parents, that they can separate and stay connected. This will greatly impact an adult's personal pattern of dealing with loss and of learning what it means—a broader world in which their relationships expand, or a lonely world void of deep connection.

Midlife: Midlife is indeed a time of both grief and awakening. A time of assessing the first half of life—what was accomplished, what remains to be done. Those in midlife stand again at a point of transition between adulthood and remaining stages of life—death rises into consciousness as they come to terms with their own mortality. Last gasps of youth are rampant in the form of affairs, sports cars—fleeting attempts at recapturing a feeling of youth under siege, despite ever-growing biological evidence that it's slipping away. The empty-nest syndrome, with its incumbent feelings of a loss of place and purpose, can leave midlifers feeling that the familiar routine and underpinnings of life have dropped out from beneath them.

Passing through a healthy, conscious grieving process helps make this a productive rather than a destructive passage. If there is unresolved grief from earlier life, it is likely to come home to roost at this stage and beg for resolution. There is still plenty of time to explore roles that have gone unexplored, to live out unlived aspirations, but there is a growing awareness that time is limited. At all of these stages, there is a heightened risk of depression. When this depression is seen as a natural part of the grief process over the loss attendant upon transition and change, it can be worked with toward resolution rather than becoming an imbedded life position.

Retirement: Waxing and waning roles are most clearly identifiable in this stage of life. The role of the worker, for example, is waning, while the role of retiree is waxing. Within each of these are many subroles. In the worker, there may be the subroles of planner, speaker, writer, seller, administrator, etc. One task at this stage is to analyze the roles that the retiree might desire to continue in some form and those the person is content to let wane. The role of speaker, for instance, can become a part of a retiree's schedule as a consultant or volunteer. There will be a grief process attached to losing certain roles but if it can be worked through successfully, retirees ought to be able to rebalance their role repertoire, translating pleasurable roles into a new arena, letting less desirable roles fade out and exploring new roles that may add to quality living, such as grandparent, mentor and spiritual seeker. This is a life transition that gives rise to what Erikson calls a "life review" or a looking back on life and assessing its value, its gains and losses, successes and failures, strengths and weaknesses, and fitting it into an overall picture. It includes both grief and celebration. Erikson sees the task of this stage as wisdom versus despair, a time when a person can examine his or her personal growth, learning and meaning, which prepares the person to meet the ultimate challenge, the transition of death, with equanimity rather than despair.

PART III

The Effect of Trauma on Relationships

Aloys Wach

The Resonance of Traum

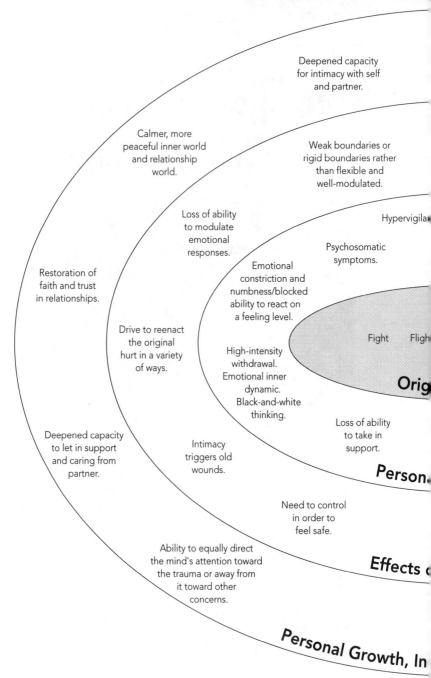

Deepened capacity
for intimacy with self
and partner.

Calmer, more
peaceful inner world
and relationship
world.

Weak boundaries or
rigid boundaries rather
than flexible and
well-modulated.

Loss of ability
to modulate
emotional
responses.

Hypervigila

Psychosomatic
symptoms.

Restoration of
faith and trust
in relationships.

Emotional
constriction and
numbness/blocked
ability to react on
a feeling level.

Drive to reenact
the original
hurt in a variety
of ways.

High-intensity
withdrawal.
Emotional inner
dynamic.
Black-and-white
thinking.

Fight   Fligh

Orig

Deepened capacity
to let in support
and caring from
partner.

Intimacy
triggers old
wounds.

Loss of ability
to take in
support.

Person

Need to control
in order to
feel safe.

Ability to equally direct
the mind's attention toward
the trauma or away from
it toward other
concerns.

Effects

Personal Growth, In

rom Hurt to Healing

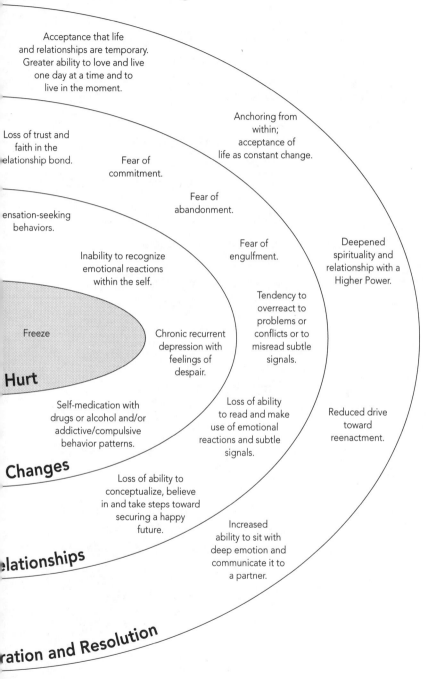

Acceptance that life and relationships are temporary. Greater ability to love and live one day at a time and to live in the moment.

Loss of trust and faith in the elationship bond.

Fear of commitment.

Anchoring from within; acceptance of life as constant change.

Fear of abandonment.

ensation-seeking behaviors.

Inability to recognize emotional reactions within the self.

Fear of engulfment.

Deepened spirituality and relationship with a Higher Power.

Tendency to overreact to problems or conflicts or to misread subtle signals.

Freeze

Chronic recurrent depression with feelings of despair.

Hurt

Self-medication with drugs or alcohol and/or addictive/compulsive behavior patterns.

Loss of ability to read and make use of emotional reactions and subtle signals.

Reduced drive toward reenactment.

Changes

Loss of ability to conceptualize, believe in and take steps toward securing a happy future.

Increased ability to sit with deep emotion and communicate it to a partner.

elationships

ration and Resolution

And this more human love
(which will consummate itself infinitely
thoughtfully and gently, and well and clearly in binding
and loosing) will be something like that which we are
preparing with struggle and toil, the love which
consists in the mutual guarding, bordering
and saluting of two solitudes.

Rainer Maria Rilke

Like everybody who is not in love,
he imagined that one chose the person whom one
loves after endless deliberations and on the strength
of various qualities and advantages.

Marcel Proust, *Cities of the Plain*

It is sweet to mingle tears with tears;
Griefs, where they wound in solitude,
Wound more deeply.

Seneca, *Agamemnon*

He that conceals his grief finds no remedy for it.

Turkish proverb

New grief awakens the old.

English proverb

The Effect of Trauma
on Relationships

I tell you the story because I was raised
the Chinese way. I was taught to desire nothing,
to swallow other people's misery and to eat my own
bitterness and even though I taught my daughter
the opposite, still she came out the same way
—maybe it is because she was born to me
and she was born a girl and I was born to my
mother and I was born a girl, all of us like stairs,
one step after another going up going down
but always going the same way. But now this
cannot be this not knowing what you're worth—
this not begin with you—my mother not
know her worth until too late—too late for
her but not for me—now we will
see if not too late for you.

AMY TAN, *THE JOY LUCK CLUB*
A CONVERSATION BETWEEN ROSIE AND HER MOTHER

Here I Go Again: When the Survivor
Enters an Intimate Relationship

Intimate relationships in the present mirror the psychological/emotional world of intimate relationships from the past. The person who grew up in a home where problems were not openly worked through lacks a model of how to solve problems and work through conflict. When the lessons learned on how to be intimate are not conducive to creating intimacy, it is difficult to sustain such relationships later on in life. In the family where trauma has occurred and not been resolved, the lessons learned are not always helpful in building the skills needed to be intimate. Skills will then need to be built oftentimes from scratch, even going against the tide of what feels familiar.

When, as adults, we enter intimate relationships without a willingness to resolve old grief, recognize the effects of early childhood traumas, work through those traumas and learn relationship skills, we run the risk of setting ourselves up for failure and acting out pain in our current relationship. Intimacy brings up in our memory bank all that we learned and stored on that subject. It calls to our most vulnerable young self, to the child who lives within us. When two adults try to be intimate, the children they once were are called to the stage of the relationship; mysteriously they come forward along with the feeling, thinking and behavior that they experienced as children. The grown man who as a little boy learned not to share his vulnerable feelings will find it very hard to do that in an intimate adult relationship. The grown woman who learned to please others and deny her own desires will likely continue that pattern in her adult relationships. These qualities are largely socialized and common to many people. If you add the fallout of trauma with profound loss of trust and faith, you have a potent cocktail for intimacy problems later in life. All intimate partnerships are a subtle and complicated balance of meeting deep needs for nurturance and acting out hungers and aggressions in the personality. A relationship needs to have a bond of trust that can hold these hungers and aggressions so that each couple can establish their own unique pattern of successful relating. No two relationships are alike, nor should they be. Each couple needs to find its own equilibrium.

Otto Kernberg, M.D., psychiatrist and psychologist, describes this aspect of intimate relationships: Unconsciously, an equilibrium is established by means of which the partners complement each other's traumas, issues and patterns from the past, and this tends to cement the relationship in new, unpredictable ways. Descriptively, we find that couples in their intimacy interact in many small, "crazy" ways. Relationships need not be perfect or meet some image of pop-psychological wellness to be functional and healthy. Each couple has what psychoanalyst B.L. Green calls a "private madness" through which they maintain that precarious bond and balance that allow for a couple's survival. They learn each other's signals, release petty aggressions, play games and generally provide the partnership with an elasticity that allows the intensity of intimacy to exist over time. When, however, pathological dynamics or roles get fixed and inflexible—for example, the abused son becomes the abusing husband or the frustrated daughter becomes the relentlessly critical spouse—then the trauma dominates too fully and the relationship may fall apart under the strain.

Intimacy Skills

Intimacy is rarely black and white—rather, it is shades of gray in a constantly changing climate of closeness. Compromise and sharing, accurately reading nuance and subtle meaning without catastrophizing and overreacting, are intimacy skills. Maintaining a sense of self while sharing the self-space of another is part of a successful close relationship. In order to do this, one needs, as Socrates said long ago, to "know thyself." Until this is accomplished, it is hardly possible to know another because knowing the self provides the frame of reference for extending that knowledge to another person. We must have enough within the self in order to have something to give away. Otherwise, the bending and adjusting involved in shared intimate space feel too threatening. We feel if we give a part of ourselves, we are losing it forever, turning it over to another person and losing control.

In fact, intimacy requires a delicate balance between having and giving, standing firm and bending, allowing and maintaining. People who have adopted either rigid or co-dependent relationship styles, in which they are either fused with another person or withdrawn, have trouble staying in a shared emotional climate. If intimacy tends to make them feel claustrophobic, they may see the solution as an escape out of the relationship altogether. On the other hand, if intimacy triggers abandonment fears, they may fuse with their partner because feeling like a separate person arouses their fear of being left. They have trouble understanding how to take space for themselves, give space to another and still stay connected to another person. This is what a trauma survivor loses by being traumatized: the trust and inner balance necessary to allow himself or herself to be a separate person meeting individual needs both within and outside of the partnership, while still staying connected in the overall context of the relationship.

Why Do I Choose the Partners I Choose? The Distorted Inner World

Object relations theory generally holds that we learn how to relate through our early family relationships, referred to as object relationships. We then internalize those relationships, where they form an internal representation of our relationship world or object world. It is this representation within us that we draw on throughout life in forming subsequent relationships. What was the quality of these attachments? Were they close, distant, fused, remote, comfortable or constantly in an anxious state, and how does that impact the way that we engage in relationships today?

Trauma distorts the internal and external relationship worlds of the survivor. Feelings are fused. "Love and violence, sexuality and aggression can become fused together in the mind of the victim of trauma. Having witnessed or experienced violence at home, the child has only maladaptive alternatives in the effort of mastering the terrifying feelings" (van der Kolk, 1987, p. 137). Children attempt to stay safe through the unconscious use of childhood defenses. They may identify with their aggressor and deny their own vulnerability, or identify with the role of a victim who is in need of protection but feels too vulnerable and at risk to be intimate. If they deny their vulnerability, they may live this out in adult relationships, acting tough, distant and impenetrable. If they identify with the victim role, they may constantly be asking others for support or protection and appear vulnerable, while at the same time they push true intimacy away because it frightens them and feels dangerous or risky.

The choice of a partner motivated unconsciously by efforts to resolve these emotional problems often re-creates the original traumatic situation. The repetitive quality of these kinds of violent and abusive relationships "suggests that identification with the aggressor is embedded in the compulsion to repeat the trauma. Repetitive patterns in intra-familial violence are well known; the woman who returns again and again to her abusive mate; the man who reenacts his own childhood sexual victimization by molesting his own children or by being victimized or the victimizer in homosexual encounters; the sexually abused adolescent girl who turns to promiscuity and prostitution" (van der Kolk, 1987, p. 138).

Other factors reinforce the power of identification. Traumatic bonding results from the utter dependency of a terrorized person on an assailant and the resulting pathological identification wherein the victim feels benignly—or even adoringly—toward his or her perpetrator. "In families where maltreatment is common, dependency is intensified because the child or adolescent has been deprived of the opportunity to develop skills and to function effectively in the world at large. Many battered women are prevented from leaving their abusive husbands and lovers by learned helplessness and low self-esteem, as well as economic dependency and social isolation" (van der Kolk, 1987, p. 138). Thus, traumatic relationship patterns are self-perpetuating—that is, we choose the very situation that we may consciously wish to avoid because unconsciously, it is deeply familiar. In the identical way that we reach toward the same foods that we often ate as a child, we reach toward familiar flavors in relationship dynamics.

We choose a partner not just with our eyes and conscious minds but from the indelible pattern and fabric of relationship imprinted on our unconscious. With uncanny accuracy we reach out toward those qualities we recognize and know, so an aspect of choice is the familiar. Within that framework of the familiar lie the possibilities on the one hand for comfort and connection, and on the other for meeting up with the fears and demons dormant in our unconscious. This is precisely why our choice of partner creates an opportunity for healing. If we choose a person who re-creates a past wound—for example, the son of a critical mother choosing a critical wife—we have another opportunity to master the initial hurt. Whereas once the son was powerless and vulnerable in the face of his mother's harangue, he is now a grown man. If he becomes conscious of what happens to him on a deeper level when his wife criticizes him, he has an opportunity to heal an old wound rather than reenact it by shutting down and withdrawing, or by mindlessly counterattacking. He can let the child within him finally put words to his inner experience, bringing it from a frozen, lifeless state into an alive and feeling one—from silence into voice.

Our choices of partners are not random. They are, in this sense, two people's unfinished selves seeking completion, but the completion they seek is in reality an attempt to see the self more fully. They are not two halves making a whole but two selves in progress toward each becoming whole so that they can, as Rainer Maria Rilke puts it, become "guardians of each other's solitudes . . .," partners in their mutual soulmaking.

Learned Helplessness: Can I Really Have a Successful Relationship?

Trauma survivors learned a powerful lesson. They were helpless in the face of a threat, whether that threat was an earthquake, sexual abuse, verbal or physical violence, or neglect. Survivors may learn "I can do nothing to stop the earth from moving, control beatings, prevent the unwanted sexual attention, explain or vindicate myself, or get the love and attention I so desperately need. My wish to make things better is only that, a wish, and try as I might I cannot translate that wish into a reality." Later in life, survivors understandably have trouble feeling that they can translate any wish into reality, be it a wish for a career, a family or a sane and healthy relationship. They stand helpless in front of their own life decisions, living out again and again their learned helplessness or their belief that try as they might, nothing they can do will make a difference.

In the arena of intimacy, they may lack an ability to modulate their involvement in intimate relationships. Trauma survivors lose the ability to modulate emotion. Later, in intimate relationships, they tend to want an all-or-nothing response, hyperconnection or disconnection, becoming either indiscriminately

involved or rejecting and shunning contact. They lack boundaries or an ability to tailor the amount of contact or intimacy
to their particular needs and desires since they were not able
to manage or affect the degree of intensity of their earlier contact. New relationships may be either idealized or hated (splitting); they may react to new relationships as they did to old
ones, alternately hating the person who is hurting them or
idealizing the person as a way of creating a false sense of safety.
The idealization serves to get them through, but keeps them
from the pain of knowing their own inner truth and feeling
their own inner fear. It is a childlike defense at feeling afraid
and vulnerable, or of accepting that the person or the world
they love and trust can also behave in ways that will hurt them.
Consider George's story.

George was married twice. He believes his first marriage was
to a thoroughly nice woman, and he regrets that his addiction to
drugs and alcohol never gave the relationship a chance. The second was an attempt to replace the loss of the first. Rather than
grieve his loss of the marriages, and before that his loss of his
mother to depression, a physical handicap and an early death,
George tried to fill the hole with another person. Unfortunately,
this meant that the current relationship had to be not only a
workable relationship in and of itself, but it had to be wonderful
enough to make up for the loss of the previous ones. George felt
resentment and despair because his relationships consistently fell
short of his needs, alternating with an almost euphoric feeling
that this was the relationship that would get his life to work. In
truth, no relationship could have taken away his pain. A small
disappointment for George could leave him wanting to dump
the whole relationship. Alternatively, feeling close to someone
made him want to immediately have a child and be a family.
Taking the steps to build a relationship—rather than to have it
all at once or get rid of it—was difficult for George.

When George talked about getting married for the third time, his commitment phobia made the words catch in his throat. I suppose, at first glance, it seems odd that someone so afraid of commitment would continually take the walk to the altar, but for George it was just this fear that drove him repeatedly to attempt to master it. He said he was afraid he'd wake up one morning and discover he had fallen out of love. Apparently, no one ever told him that this would be perfectly normal, that married couples fall in and out of love several times a week—that that's what commitment is all about, why it's necessary. Commitment scared George because he saw it in black-and-white terms, he was in love or out of love, he cared completely or not at all. Modulating feelings can take all sorts of forms, including allowing for the ebb and flow natural to any relationship.

Additionally George engaged in high-risk behaviors such as unprotected sex. This came to a head when he thought he had impregnated his girlfriend and we were able to examine what was underneath his having high-risk sex. Thrill-seeking, high-risk behavior allowed him to override the fear and pain that came up for him when he contemplated marriage. It provided him with the heightened intensity that trauma survivors look for in order to pull themselves out of emotional shutdown and to feel alive and emotionally connected. He was also responding to a deep need for nurturing and family, but he was unconsciously driven to create it instantly, avoiding the step-by-step process of building a relationship that could sustain intimacy and child-rearing.

Once George identified this, it took him literally only a matter of weeks to turn his behavior around. He was then able to make plans to live with his chosen one and give the relationship a chance to work, to rise or fall on its own merit. As his new relationship progressed, he brought the issues into the therapy group that would have made him want to leave his relationship. When he, for example, had a fight with his partner, he often fell into shame and self-doubt, which turned quickly into doubting the relationship. These feelings kept a conflict going and made it difficult for him to let it go and move on. He felt guilty and feared that if he couldn't resolve each and every issue, there was something fundamentally flawed in the relationship. He came to see that all relationships have flaws and that working them out occurred slowly and over time. Once he gained this perspective, he could let problems arise, work through them with his partner as well as they could for the time being, then let them go and return to comfortable relating. This gave his relationship some breathing space, which allowed the parts that were working well to strengthen, which made the whole relationship more comfortable to live in.

He surprised himself, I think, that he could successfully talk and work through problems when he was not burdened with the expectation that the relationship had to function "perfectly" in order to be considered good. In this way he and his partner were able to use their relationship to rebuild intimacy skills that had previously been undermined and to accept their ups and downs as part of what constituted their particular relationship. They no longer conjectured that conflict meant that their relationship was profoundly flawed; it did not have to end. This freed them up to experience the love, understanding and comfort that characterized their relationship much of the time. In short, they were learning to modulate intense emotion and live within a normal range rather than punish themselves and the relationship for falling short of an unrealistic, idealized image.

Traumatic Bonds: Why Do I Keep Choosing the "Wrong" People?

As we have been discussing, it is a disquieting truth that people who have grown up in abusive families often choose partners with whom they re-create the very dynamics that brought them pain in their early relationships.

One of the reasons that trauma survivors form relationships with people who treat them abusively, such as a woman who was abused as a child choosing a husband who is abusive to her, is a phenomenon called *traumatic bonding*. The classic example of traumatic bonding is the concentration camp victim who adores her captor and tries to please him and gain his favor. Traumatic bonding, according to Jon G. Allen, Ph.D., of The Menninger Clinic, "requires two conditions: there must be an imbalance of power, and the victim must be isolated from other forms of support. The battering husband, for example, intimidates and physically overpowers his spouse, and he jealously keeps her captive by forbidding outside relationships and frightening others away. Why doesn't the battered woman just leave? Plainly, there may be dire circumstances. For example, her husband may threaten to pursue and assault her (or their children) if she leaves. Also, she may be totally financially dependent on him" (Allen, 1996).

A child who has grown up with an abandoning or abusive father has formed a deep attachment bond with that relationship dynamic. When she chooses a partner later in life, she will very possibly choose what feels familiar, what feels like home.

Many persons with a history of trauma have experienced a destructive combination of injury and neglect, resulting in alternating working models of relationship: one model entails an emotionally intense, for example, violent sense of relatedness. Another model entails a painful sense of isolation and disconnection. Such persons may not have solid working models for benign relationships. When they are treated with kindness, compassion and respect, they feel anxious and guilty. Unlike those who have been well cared for, they have no working model to encompass such benign experience. They cannot relate to it, and they have difficulty responding appropriately to it. In addition, a seemingly calm and stable relationship, such as cultivated in psychotherapy, may be experienced as boring, empty, or unfulfilling. Missing the intense contact, the patient may increasingly feel disconnected and anxious. Paradoxically, an abusive interaction may diminish the painful isolation by providing a sense of connection that is elusive in a calmer relationship. Or, in psychotherapy, the patient may generate repeated crises to evoke alarm and feel reconnected by the therapist's intense concern (or frustration) (Allen, 1996).

Children who grow up in homes with abuse, psychological illness or addiction fulfill the conditions for forming a traumatic bond. A natural power imbalance exists between a parent and child, and a hurting child is often isolated from other forms of support because of family secrecy and shame. This is how a traumatic bond forms. Later, as adults, these children unconsciously choose the same sort of relationship because that is what they have learned intimacy *feels* like. When they look for adult intimacy, they look for what they knew. A comfortable, calm relationship can feel boring. They miss the intensity that was part of the traumatic bond. They live out a pattern of connection and disconnection, alternating between withdrawing into their own inner world and, when that feels lonely, regaining a sense of connectedness by picking a fight or getting involved in some form of intense relating that provides temporary relief from their feeling of isolation.

Brain Scripts

Recent brain research has helped us understand that the behavior that we experience as a child becomes a script literally imprinted on the brain, and we operate from the contents of that script throughout life, choosing life circumstances that match up with the information we have stored in that "brain file." Thus, in relationships, we are likely to choose what we know because that is what we have stored in our filing system on that subject.

Knowing this, we can use these repetitions to understand where our inner work lies. The problems we continually repeat that get us into trouble send up a red flag, marking the spot of earlier pain. There are two ways to go through these repetitions. In reenactment, we repeat the experience with no awareness of what we are doing, drawing no meaningful connections between the unhealthy dynamic in the present and the earlier childhood experience of pain or alienation. This is *retraumatizing*. It re-creates the previous stress or abuse and reenacts it. Such people may go through life feeling like a victim, like they get all the bad luck, like nothing ever goes right for them. It is a cycle in which people are set up and set themselves up for being a victim over and over again, for being retraumatized in the same way that they were previously traumatized.

The other way to go through repetitions uses the current life experience to make the feelings from the past conscious, to once again be willing to sit with the feelings that an early experience from youth produced so that the survivor can understand, heal those feelings and open up for new corrective experiences. Our earlier couple, Bill and Connie, unconsciously retraumatized each other by confusing old pain from the past with painful relationship dynamics in the present.

Bill, in his relationship with Connie, was hypervigilant around the subjects of anger and humiliation. His most painful moments with his mother were when she was angry. Rather than express anger directly, she humiliated Bill as a way of releasing her aggressive feelings toward him. If you had asked her if she felt aggressive feelings, she would have been completely out of touch with them and surprised by the insinuation, which is precisely why the humiliation and criticism were so powerful—they were made more potent with unclaimed, unacknowledged anger. If and when Connie looked angry, Bill imagined that her hostility was far greater than it actually was, and he alternately felt demeaned and furious at what he perceived to be Connie's negative feelings toward him.

Because of Bill's unconscious fears around Connie's anger, he continually provoked it. Though at first glance this may seem contradictory, it is a common behavior to unconsciously participate in re-creating the behavior we fear the most, in an unconscious attempt to gain some sense of relief from feelings of fear and anxiety. In this way, Bill set himself up to be retraumatized. Once he understood his role in creating this dynamic and became willing to get in touch with the pain he felt from his mother's anger and humiliation, he began to notice his own emotional bind. Later, when he felt triggered by Connie's anger, he took a break until he again felt calm enough inside to share his real, vulnerable feelings rather than becoming defensive and attack Connie, he was able to detach the shadow of his angry mother from Connie's face. This also gave Connie the opportunity to feel less accused and vilified by Bill, which made her less defensive or likely to lash out in anger, which would have reignited the whole dynamic.

Few of us like emotional pain. But feeling the pain is actually the quickest way out of it. It is necessary, though, not only to feel the pain but to then make the appropriate connection, as Bill did between the old hurt and the current life situation. Without making these connections the full insight doesn't occur, and insight is a first step toward changing the behavior. So the life circumstance that is problematic can actually give us an opportunity to redo the past—doing, undoing and redoing. *Doing* the repeated behavior, *undoing* or feeling the feelings underneath the behavior related to the original hurt, and *redoing,* doing it differently, learning and practicing new ways of being. This is the process through which victims become the victors, recognizing their own pattern of repetition, confronting its root cause, exploring the feelings and the meaning they made out of it and came to live by, then changing the dysfunctional for more functional, satisfying behavior.

Stress experienced early in life can alter the way we respond to stress as adults.

> Another study of the brain's makeup reported last June [1995] at the meeting of the American Psychiatric Association, provides some of the earliest proof that stress can physically alter people. With magnetic resonance imaging, researchers took pictures of the brains of 38 women, 20 with a documented history of sexual abuse, 18 without. Among those women sexually abused as children, the researchers discovered, the hippocampus is actually smaller than normal. A tiny seahorse-shaped structure in the middle of the brain, the hippocampus is partially responsible for storing short-term memory. It is activated by some of the same neurohormones released during stress. "What we are seeing," says Murray Stein, Ph.D., of the University of California at San Diego, "is evidence that psychological stress can change the brain's makeup" (Carpi, 1996).

It is no wonder, then, that adults who experienced stress and trauma as children overrespond to stress as adults by becoming easily triggered into irrational emotions relevant to the original trauma, but irrelevant to the current situation; or by becoming hypervigilant or reverting to childhood defenses from emotional pain.

Relationship Shadows

Trauma survivors often store the wounds from their painful experiences in what Carl Jung would call their shadow sides. The shadow is an unacknowledged part of a person that is hidden from the self, but as this aspect of self continues to be hidden, to be cast into a dark place in the psyche, it gains rather than loses power. The more unconscious we are of what lies in the contents of the shadow, the greater the shadow's power to choose with whom we will have a relationship.

Connie's father was both alcoholic and sexually abusive. He was also her greatest ally and her most bonded relationship within the family. As a child, it was impossible for her to balance and integrate these two opposing aspects of her father. On the one hand, he was the ideal father, anticipating her thoughts and responding to her on a truly heartfelt level. On the other hand, his drinking and sexual invasion were deeply frightening. He was often lost to her for days or even weeks at a time during his binges, or else terrifying her with his inappropriate sexual attention.

During these difficult periods, Connie lived on her memories. She waited for her "good daddy" to sober up and return. Though she feared deep down she couldn't rely on him, she acted as if she could. After all, if she were to admit to herself how sick her father really was, where would she go? Whom would she turn to? Her mother had long since tuned out and survived by structuring an absorbing life outside of the family, and in which Connie played no role. The message she got from her mother was, "You can live here, but don't need anything from me. I have enough on my plate. I can't handle any more from you." In addition, Connie's mother felt an unspoken envy at the intimacy and attention her husband gave to their daughter. Connie's father, sick though he was, was still her most caring and concerned parent. Consequently, Connie idealized her father and, when he died, the things that frightened her about him got relegated to a place in her mind where they felt more manageable—that is, to her shadow.

For Connie, it would have been too scary to admit how much her father's behavior frightened her, for a couple of reasons: one, her fear of abandonment ("If he's not here, then no one is.") and two, her identification with him ("If he's a mess, then what does that say about me?"). When Connie reached the age to choose a husband, her shadow, as well as her conscious mind, chose. Her traumatic bond with her father was activated. Her conscious mind chose a nice, loving man; her shadow chose a man who had problems with repressed anger, sexual issues, and alcohol and drug abuse, though he was sober in AA at the time of their marriage. Then she lived out exactly the dynamic she had learned, which was to adore and idealize the qualities that made her feel safe and pretend the qualities that scared her weren't there. She split off the frightening parts from conscious awareness and continued to hide them in the shadow. When Bill behaved in ways that triggered old fears, she then saw him as all bad; the shadow temporarily emerged and she saw the situation as black and white. The diverging qualities of her father that she could not integrate in the past became the diverging qualities of Bill that she could not integrate in her present. During a conflict, she projected the painful contents of her shadow onto Bill, and the past and the present became indistinguishable within her. At those moments, it was impossible for her to resolve a conflict with him because she could not tell the difference between Bill and her father on an emotional level.

Bill, on the other hand, had the mirror image of Connie's past. He had been closest to his mother, who was an alcoholic. His primary identification had been with her, while his relationship with his father had been much more distant and filled with envy and competition over his intimacy with his mother. When Connie, who had her own problems with anger, acted in ways that alarmed Bill and reminded him of his mother's drunkenness (which he repressed in the same way Connie had her father's), Bill pulled away, seeing Connie as all bad, clingy, difficult and to be avoided. For a while the couple struggled along—getting on well, getting triggered, distancing, getting upset, then reuniting through sex, time or tearful apology, withdrawal versus intense connection. Eventually, the strain became problematic.

Fortunately for Connie and Bill, they sought therapy at this point rather than divorce. In therapy, I helped the couple look at how their own histories were getting projected onto each other, making it impossible to separate their past from their present, so that they could successfully resolve a conflict. They each had significant grief work to do—Connie for the loss of the father she so needed to depend upon, as well as her sorrow over not having a mother she could really turn to in need; Bill over the loss of the sober mother he so deeply loved and identified with, and his sadness at his years spent trying to understand how to become a man without the attentive guidance of his father. Connie and Bill each chose a partner who mirrored their own history both consciously and unconsciously; they made each other feel safe and insecure, connected and alone, just as they had felt as children.

Both Bill and Connie were also the idealized partner by their opposite-sex parent. The estrangement that their parents felt from one another made them seek out in their relationships with their children qualities that they found missing in their spouses. The result was that both Bill and Connie felt chosen in a special way to fulfill their parents' need and guilty for this special attention. Part of their healing was to triumph over this oedipal guilt by choosing one another and living a happy life.

When they got the help that they needed to understand rather than blindly reenact their past wounds, they helped each other to heal rather than retraumatize each other. Eventually they were able to create a deep and lasting bond that had within it all of the innocent love that had been a part of their earlier parent bonds. They came to understand how to use each other as vehicles for healing, comforting each other when wounds erupted, sharing their vulnerable hurt feelings rather than wounding each other more. Though they had slips back into their old dynamics, these episodes were farther apart and of shorter duration, and as they practiced new behaviors they strengthened healthier patterns of relating.

How Do Trauma and Stress Get Played Out in Relationships?

One effect of childhood trauma is that we become hypervigilant. Our "stress sensors" work on overdrive, attempting to ferret out impending danger so that we can avoid it and stay safe. Unfortunately, this kind of hypervigilance actually creates stress. A person who goes through life ready to react is not really able to live comfortably and will tend to overinterpret ordinary life events that another person might dismiss or ignore. The person's overreaction to potential stress can actually keep him or her in a state of hyperarousal or chronic stress.

Traumatized people tend to seek each other out for intimate relationships—their insides match. It is an unconscious attraction but all the more problematic and powerful for this very reason: They don't know what issues are the source of attraction. Connie had an alcoholic father and an emotionally remote mother; Bill had an alcoholic mother and a cold and distant father. Each of them came from successful families that went from being stars on the social scene to being devastated by alcoholism and divorce during Bill's and Connie's teenage years.

Both Bill and Connie were the chosen favorite of the opposite-sex, alcoholic parent, and the whole family knew it. Each of them stood in as a surrogate partner for that parent who was dissatisfied and estranged from his or her partner. The inner worlds of Bill and Connie were mirror images of each other. Depending on the couple, this can be a recipe for disaster or a recipe for success.

In the case of Connie and Bill, it worked out—they felt unconsciously doubled by each other, as if each of them "had been there." The pain that they could not articulate, they could sense in each other, and it gave them enough feeling of safety so that they were able to do the extensive emotional work necessary to heal.

It is no surprise that Bill and Connie were constantly triggering each other. They fought a lot, which is where they were when they came to see me. One of their core dynamics was distancer/pursuer; Connie feared abandonment, Bill feared engulfment. When Connie felt Bill was becoming remote, she came closer. As she came closer, he felt claustrophobic and pulled away, which made Connie pursue him further—then Bill distanced all the more. When Connie collapsed from exhaustion and stopped pursuing, Bill came toward her. At the center of this dance was their deep fear of intimacy. As the ice around their hearts melted in the hot furnace of intimacy, their old hurts were warmed up—they could feel them again, and feeling them hurt.

"He feels remote to me," said Connie, "as if he won't connect to me or to the children for any prolonged length of time. He's great for short spurts, but then it seems as if he has to get out, to escape, and I resent his pulling back."

"Connie's neediness makes me feel as if she wants to swallow me whole. I want to peel her off. I need to get away."

Neither Connie nor Bill knew how to be intimate without fusing or cutting off, so their closeness was overcloseness, which made them seek distance for relief. This didn't give either of them the breathing space they needed to be close in a way that allowed for normal personal boundaries. They were one, or they were strangers. The traumatic bonds formed in their childhood left them with high intensity or withdrawal as blueprints for relationships. When the intensity got too hot, they withdrew. Bill physically left so that he could get in touch with himself again. Connie fused, disappearing not outside the relationship but inside of it, imploding, reaching out with tears or anger to draw him back and reduce her abandonment anxiety.

Another way they connected was through fighting, blaming, blowing up, then reconnecting after they had, at least for the moment, given vent to the pain they carried around. Like so many trauma survivors, they had lost the ability to modulate emotion, to move in and out of emotionally charged spaces without blowing up, disassociating or shutting down.

Separating the Past from the Present: Understanding Transference in Relationships

In order to stop the compulsion to continually reenact painful relationship dynamics, transferences need to be identified and worked through. Connie transferred or projected the pain she experienced with her father (and mother) onto Bill, while Bill transferred the pain he experienced with his mother (and father) onto Connie.

The essential characteristic of transference is experiencing feelings toward a person in the present that actually don't apply to that person, but to another person from a past relationship. It is reacting to that person in the present as if he or she were the person from the past. Ralph Greenson describes transference with his client when the client is kept waiting for a therapy appointment as follows:

> Transference reactions are always inappropriate. They may be so in the quality, quantity or duration of the reaction. The transference reaction is unsuitable in its current context; but it once was an appropriate reaction to that situation. Just as ill-fitting as transference reactions are to a person in the present, they fit snugly to someone in the past. This is an [example of

an] inappropriate reaction for a thirty-five-year-old intelligent and cultured woman, but her associations lead to a situation with this set of feelings and fantasies. She recalls her reaction as a child, waiting for her father to come to her room to kiss her goodnight. She always had to wait a few minutes because he made it a rule to kiss her younger sister goodnight first. Then she reacted by tears, anger, jealousy fantasies, precisely what she is now experiencing with me. Her reactions are appropriate for a five-year-old girl, but obviously not fitting for a thirty-five-year-old woman. The key to understanding this behavior is recognizing that it is a repetition of the past, i.e., a transference reaction. Transference reactions are essentially repetitions of a past . . . relationship. . . . it is this fact that a piece of behavior repeats something in the past that makes it likely to be inappropriate in the present (Greenson, 1967, p. 152, 153).

When transferences rule our current life relationships, we are unable to get a clear picture of ourselves or our relationships. People in the present are confused unconsciously with people from the past, and our reactions to them are colored by past experience. We can, however, learn to use our transferences as indicators of where our inner work lies. When we see ourselves having reactions to people that seem inappropriate or unusually intense, we can take time to look at where they may be coming from. Any present-day situation we consistently overreact to tells us something about ourselves to which we need to listen. No one knows our history as well as we do if we allow ourselves to see it. Transference reactions give us a way to better know ourselves, to accept our history and to cleanse ourselves of aspects of our history that impede our living fully and happily in the present. When we come to understand the source of the transference, we experience a shift in awareness; perhaps as in the case study, we might gain compassion for the little girl who lay anxiously waiting to be kissed goodnight. We may come to realize that we were not unloved, but a situation poorly handled made us feel unloved. The truth is oftentimes less painful than our repeated transference reaction. The very pain we were avoiding can hurt less than the messes we create with our inappropriate reactions. Transference reactions need to be understood so that present-day relationships are not ruled and run by unresolved pain from the past.

How Projected Pain Turns into Caretaking

In projective identification, we take a part of ourselves about which we carry deep unresolved anxiety and project it onto another person, seeing it as if it belonged to them and not to us. Once we unconsciously project this part of the self onto another, we disown it and see it as being a part of that person. How many of us are the harshest disciplinarians or feel the greatest anxiety when someone else evidences feelings and behaviors that we are too ashamed to own and look at within ourselves? Once we get rid of the painful feelings by disowning them within ourselves, we can feel momentary relief because we are safe from our own dark side ("He is angry, not me"). Alternatively, we can complicate things further and set about fixing in another person what we unconsciously know needs fixing in ourselves—something we cannot consciously admit.

Then we project pieces of ourselves where they do not belong, disowning them within ourselves and seeing them as belonging exclusively to someone else. This disrupts our own boundaries and we lose contact with who we really are. We need to own these pieces of ourselves and to work through them in order to be more fully alive and integrated. For the person being projected on, a block is placed in front of that person's own personal growth because he or she is being asked to accept something that person doesn't necessarily own. For the projector, it is an attempt to stay away from the self. The projector identifies a quality in another person that the projector does not want to acknowledge exists within himself or herself. In the case of care-taking, the projector may then go about correcting the problem in the other person in a variety of ways.

Projective identification enables projectors to psychically place their inner tension and complex in someone else, where it may or may not exist. The "correcting" of it may take different forms. Projectors may be harsh with other people, attempting "to save them from harm" or "get them to see what they are doing" so that they will not run into the same trouble that the projectors unconsciously feel that they have had. Another form the caretaking may take is when projectors are overly anxious or solicitous about perceived defects in other people. For people being projected on, this may be experienced as a boundary inva-sion, something that makes them feel uncomfortable because they are being asked to own something that they do not feel is actually in them, and on top of it they are getting compassion and warmth for identifying with a problem with which they do not actually identify. This puts them into a real dilemma. Do they embrace the warmth and compassion that feels good and, in a sense, ignore their true inner reading, or do they stand up for who they feel they really are and risk offending the person delivering warmth and compassion? When a projective identifi-cation is unconscious, projectors truly feel that what they are see-ing is real, and they may resent being told that they are wrong. In fact, they have trouble taking it in. They may simply view it as stubbornness or even meanness on the part of the other per-son. The bind for the person who is the object of the caretak-ing is impossible. It is a lose–lose situation. Caretaking, though it masquerades as concern for another person, is all too often an attempt to lessen the caretaker's own anxiety by displacing it onto someone else.

An example of this can be seen in the manner in which Laura relates to her husband. Laura's way of coping with her pain was to, in a sense, deny its presence within herself, identify it in another person, and then attempt to fix and comfort that other person. Her sensitivity to her husband bordered on hypersensitivity. If her anxiety level was high, rather than identify herself as anxious, she identified anxiety in him, then tried to help him with it. Caretaking is by nature a denial of self, but the insidiousness of it is that caretakers see in another person what they are unable to see or own within themselves. It is confusing both for the caretaker and the person being caretaken. Laura's husband, Jim, felt a weird combination of comfort and cloying—feeling both understood and missed altogether. Laura was confused because she actually thought she was helping Jim in a selfless manner, and when her attempts to help were met with a combination of gratitude and revulsion, she also felt both appreciated and misunderstood.

Caretaking, however, is not necessarily a selfless action. Instead, it can be about the caretaker's needs to reduce their own anxiety and pain by externalizing it—projecting it onto another and fixing it there. When Laura's attempts to "help" Jim were not appreciated, she felt rejected. She could not see that it didn't necessarily feel good to him to be comforted when she felt the need to comfort. Laura really needed to learn to receive comfort within herself, but first she had to do the grief work that she had been avoiding, that was blocking her own ability to take in support. One of her problems in working through grief was that she was afraid that if she got angry with her parents, even in therapy, or let herself feel her sadness, she would lose her parents altogether.

In Laura's case, it took time to reassure her that she could be angry at the way she was treated as a child and still keep the relationships she had today. People change, parents grow as well as children, and few of us have just the same parents as adults that we had as children. In fact, grieving that old pain and hurt often improves the present-day relationship. Laura was able to do this in therapy, where it was safe, rather than with her now elderly parents, where it probably would not have worked too well. Therapy provided a safe place to work through the intense and painful irrational emotions. Later, when Laura became anxious because her intimacy with Jim felt threatening, she was able to be more open and honest about her feelings, which made her less encumbered by old pain and more able to be herself, neither the obedient little caretaker nor the resentful, angry wife. This opened the door for her to receive the support she hungered for rather than projecting that need onto someone else.

Repeating History: The Sins of the Father Are Visited upon the Son

We are most vulnerable to repeating history when we are not able to integrate, understand and consciously make our own meaning of experience. Making constructive meaning of experience is the psyche's way of learning and growing from adversity, placing it in its proper perspective. Though we may have been a victim in some circumstances, we do not need to form that self-concept.

Conscious awareness is the key to not blindly repeating history. While the feelings and behaviors attached to a particular experience remain unconscious, when we encounter a situation similar to the original one, all of the behavior and feeling attached to the original circumstance plays out again. We use a coping pattern that was designed to manage trauma or high stress, rather than one that is designed to handle the daily issues that any relationship must face. The coping pattern, while appropriate for earlier high-stress situations, is inappropriate for normal day-to-day circumstances, and only gets in the way of comfortable relating. When feelings are not fully felt or experienced, they cannot get integrated along with the thoughts and the behaviors that accompany them. Thought, feeling and behavior become separate and disconnected. In order to reconnect and integrate them, they need to be brought to a conscious level and experienced in the here and now as they were originally felt. The feeling that was repressed or dissociated from because it was too painful is the road back to integration. Once that piece of history is made conscious and felt for what it was, it can be reworked in the present, and its personal meaning can be understood.

Fear of Feeling Good:
Letting in Comfort and Support

For pleasure and inner peace to operate, the hurt that bars their entry must be cleared away. When trauma occurs, thinking and feelings get welded together. Intimacy and danger, love and pain, get carried within the mind in a fused state so that later in life when the trauma survivor encounters intimacy, for example, it may trigger fears of danger or abandonment. With this set of feelings getting constantly set off, intimate relationships come to feel like mined territory—as if the slightest misstep can lead to eruption and misunderstanding. Trauma survivors become perennially suspicious, unable to stay in the present with modulated, appropriate responses. Instead, the present is constantly being pulled at by unresolved complexes and fears that have their roots in the past. Locating the trauma or traumas that feed the paranoia is like diving for a crashed plane in a murky lake or a shadow-filled unconscious. Trauma survivors dive down and try to dredge up pieces of the wreckage one by one, hoping enough gets reassembled so that clues as to the cause of the disaster can be revealed, or they wait to see if pieces will float to the surface and provide clues as to what lies below. Clues or symptoms can be obscure. Often what looks like a piece of the wing may instead belong somewhere else. It is a search where at times all divers must depend on touch and calculated guesswork. But eventually, if trauma survivors dredge the waters long enough, most are rewarded with the truth, and once that is known, victims/survivors—whether it be of a plane crash or a painful family history—can begin to reorganize. Until enough truth is known, the psyche is somehow not at rest. Trauma survivors need to understand what happened so that they can reorder their inner world with that information in it, so that they can return to the land of the living and reintegrate the disaster in a found state within the psyche.

Oftentimes people want to skip over the second and third stages of grieving and mourning and go straight to the fourth and fifth. If this could be done, none of us would carry unresolved wounds. If we could simply go from numbness to reorganization without experiencing yearning, searching, sadness, anger and despair, there would be no need for a field of psychology or a theory of trauma or mourning. The human heart and the human psyche are far too complex to be reduced in this manner. The genesis of behavior is thought and emotion. Thought and emotion are outgrowths of the vast network of experiences and the meanings we have drawn from them. People make meaning out of traumatic situations and then live according to that meaning or interpretation. With lightning speed, the brain whizzes through its filing system and pulls out from the lake of the unconscious that stored information that matches the stimuli from the current environment. Whether the information is good or bad, helpful or distorted, is immaterial—it is the process of pulling it from its storage or continuing to repress it that is the work of the brain. What is in there is what will come up; the pain will erupt.

When pain emerges, it may be an intense feeling, a somatic response such as palm sweating or increased heart rate, or an unsettling wish to distance or dissociate from an awkward or painful situation. The illusion that a person can skip over the middle steps of mourning means skipping over the loss or trauma itself and everything attached to it. Such people are trying to write sentences in their life story without knowing the proper vocabulary—too much is missing for meaningful comprehension and resolution to take place. It is in diving into the feeling, into the lake of the unconscious, that the missing pieces are found.

Pockets of Pain

Most relationships do not fall apart in total—they fall apart in pieces. Parts of the relationship function well, while other parts are problematic, mired in sick dynamics that make the relationship feel as if it is all bad. Identifying and working with the particular part or dynamic of the relationship that has "fallen ill" can restore health to the overall relationship. No relationship is perfect, nor is that an appropriate goal. What we want to do is bring the parts of the relationship that are problematic to a conscious level, where they can be worked with and resolved so that they no longer have the power to undermine the overall health of the relationship.

People heal in layers. People are works in progress—so are relationships. Each time we recover another piece of self or another piece of the relationship, we also recover another piece of the puzzle that was missing in order to gain a clearer view and a fuller understanding of what went wrong. Then we can translate that learning onto the practical stage of living. We integrate that new learning into the self and the relationship so that we function better. Then another layer comes to the surface for reexamination. We process and resolve that, then integrate it. And so it goes: Layer by layer, sickness is removed and health is restored.

For several decades many in society have seen the solution to solving relationship problems as leaving one relationship and starting a new one. Though at times this may be necessary, all too often people learn that the same problems often surface in subsequent partnerships. Why is this? For people who have been traumatized or deeply hurt in particular areas of their personality during early childhood relationships, there is an unconscious drive to reenact that pain. Why? There are many theories on this, ranging from an attempt to master the original conflict to reenacting a script imprinted on the brain. As we discuss in this book, it is in bringing these wounded parts of self to consciousness, where they can be felt and seen for what their reality is, that healing takes place. When pain is felt rather than denied, and looked at rather than repressed, it can be seen in a new light, understood and reintegrated into the unconscious with new awareness attached. We can then engage in corrective experiences that can add new, healthier memories alongside the old ones. Thus, the power fueling the drive toward reenactment is reduced.

All this work is done layer by layer, and relationships act as the vehicle that both stimulates the old wound and gives it a place to heal. Trauma is, remember, an "interruption of the affiliative bond" or the relationship bond. It needs to be healed in a relationship. Intimate relationships then offer an opportunity for growth and healing as well as an arena for reenactment. Using relationships as a path toward personal healing gives them a spiritual focus that benefits the relationship and the people in it. Who on their death bed says they wish they'd spent a little more time at the office? It is the relationships in our lives that make life worth living, that create a heaven or a hell in our day-to-day world. Using intimate relationships as a path toward heaven rather than as a path toward hell is work that strengthens the personality, softens the heart and deepens the spirit. An important aspect of the process of healing and resolution is learning to allow life to work out, to live with peace and calm without sabotaging it because it is not familiar.

The Emotionally Resilient Couple

Working through emotional problems that a couple faces is one of the factors that produces emotional resilience. Couples have self-images as a couple as well as individually, and build shared self-esteem by facing and working with problems. Even if the problems do not get fully resolved, the act of confronting them rather than hiding from them produces strength. Other factors that produce emotional resilience in a couple are shared experience. Belonging to a church, synagogue or temple provides a sense of community and connections and offers a resource to turn to in time of need. A social network composed of extended family, couple-friends and family-friends enhances a couple's network of support. Mutual hobbies that a couple enjoys, be it moviegoing, theater, golf, or gardening add interest and entertainment to the life of the couple. Much healing takes place outside of the therapist's office and beyond conflict resolution. Couples can isolate just as individuals can, and that isolation inhibits opportunities for building a comfortable and happy relationship.

Couples also need to actively seek out and pursue both private and shared experiences. The private experiences allow each individual to pursue personal goals and pleasures and brings fresh energy into the relationship. The shared experiences bond the couple to each other as they establish an identity as a couple in the world at large. It is an act of victory to create a mutual and sustaining relationship in a world that constantly offers temptation to undermine that bond. Couples who have achieved this victory over forces that threaten its survival, from both within and outside of the relationship, develop a secure base from which to operate in life and through which to draw support and nurturance. "What we call *resilience* is turning out to be an interactive and systemic phenomenon, the product of a complex relationship of inner strengths and outer help throughout a person's life span. Resilience is not only an individual matter, it is the outward and visible sign of a web of relationships and experiences that teach people mastery, doggedness, love, moral courage and hope" (Butler, 1997, p. 25).

Fear of Success

Problems letting in the good can take a variety of forms in both intimate relationships and the workplace. Success or reaching life goals can trigger fears of letting abundance and accomplishment become real. Consider Jeff's story, and the way he accomplished his goal and achieved his dream.

Jeff finished his master's in social work last spring and gave himself the summer off before he tackled job hunting in the fall. He came to group in September and said, "I can't get out of bed, all I do is watch TV; unless I have something I absolutely have to do, I just lie there." I needed to hear more to understand the extent to which this inertia had taken over his life and how we might work with it. He went on, "I haven't worked on my résumé; the few places I've sent it to, I don't make follow-up calls—and the doctor said it's crucial that I start going to the gym for my blood pressure." This was serious. He was getting into a self-destructive pattern both physically and psychologically and it needed to change soon. "I can't ask for help. I don't know why, I just can't." I had heard this before. "Laura [a successful head-hunter] said she would help me with my résumé but I can't call her. You," he said pointing to Laura, "I can't call you." I asked him why he couldn't call her; how did the thought of calling her make him feel? "I don't know, I just can't."

We could have explored the reasons for this resistance, but Jeff is himself a therapist and one of his main defenses is intellectualization. We needed to do something else to create a therapeutic experience that would allow him to actually feel what it would be like to ask for and receive help. Trauma survivors need to learn what it feels like to take in support and love so that they will know what they are looking for in the world. Otherwise, it is as if they are thirsty but walk right by the drinking fountain because they don't know that the water in the drinking fountain will quench their thirst. They need to make that connection on a somatic level, to experience it within themselves in order for it to become real and a part of them.

I asked Jeff if he could ask someone in the group for help. "I can't, I just can't." He already knew the reasons intellectually, but his emotions were still tied up in the past. He did express that he felt supported the previous week by James. This was important because Jeff, a gay man, talks often about feeling that he can't accept support from other men, especially heterosexual men, such as James. It is my feeling that it hurts too much, that it brings up the pain of his father's lack of acceptance of him and his withdrawal of love and support throughout his life. I asked him if he would be willing to let James stand behind him for support or even put his hands on Jeff's shoulders. Jeff accepted, though he said that it felt excruciating, that he wanted to leave and was having trouble staying present. I wanted to see if Jeff could be helped by nonsexualized support from a man. He had often said that he was unable to accept that.

Next I asked Jeff to go around the group and ask each person for something specific, some tangible form of support. He began to go around the circle: "Laura, will you help me with my résumé?—I hate this—Giermo, can I talk to you? Sometimes I see you as very cool and hip and when I'm around you I feel like a nerd—this is hard—Sophie, will you encourage me to look for a job and when I change the subject bring me back to it? This feels scary," he continued. "Maya, you suggested that I might benefit if someone checked in with me to see if I had done the things I said I would do. Would you be willing to do that?—this feels really weird." And so it went. Jeff went around the room asking for support of various kinds from each group member. Anyone was free to say yes or no; it was Jeff's job only to ask. I "doubled" behind him, giving voice to what I supposed might be his inner life, to what he might be experiencing beneath the surface, constantly checking with him to see if I was on target or if he needed to correct what I was saying (a technique of psychodrama). I said, "This isn't easy. What if they say no? They're going to resent my asking. They won't want to do this," and so on. With the support of James and the "double," he was able to ask for support and to continually verbalize the feelings that asking for support brought up for him.

The next week Jeff came to group with a different look in his eyes. Over the week he had joined a gym, completed his résumé, gone to a 12-Step meeting each day and made phone calls, both personal and professional. It became clear to him that when he moves into action, it is total action, and then he feels overwhelmed and burned out and wants to collapse in bed and stay there. The classic trauma pattern—high intensity or withdrawal. We talked about how he needed to learn to ask for support and modulate his activities. His inability to do these things was a direct result of the trauma he experienced from having a cold, distant, alcoholic father whom he could never please and a mother who supported the father to the exclusion of him, and of his issues around feeling unaccepted as a gay male in his family and social network—feeling written off, categorized and marginalized. Jeff has all the right equipment for accomplishing his goals, including the training. What is missing on a deeper level is his need to learn that he doesn't have to continue the pattern of being cut off. He can get support if he can learn to take it in, and he can break down tasks into manageable pieces that he can undertake one at a time.

Two weeks after this work, Jeff came to group with the news that he had obtained a job—not only a job, but exactly the job he had wanted—not only that, but a job that had been specially created for him because this organization found him so valuable.

In the Arena of Relationships, Survivors of Psychological Trauma May:

- Avoid intimate relationships because they unconsciously fear another interruption of the affiliative bond (isolation)

- Re-create relationship dynamics that mirror their original trauma (reenactment)

- Unconsciously project unhealed pain and anger from the original trauma into present-day intimate relationships (transferences)

- Become enmeshed in intimate relationships in an unconscious attempt to protect against abandonment (fusing)

- Distance their partner when they enter a dependent relationship (withdrawal)

- Later respond to situations that trigger them by shutting down, or with an intensity of emotions appropriate to the original traumatic situation (triggering)

- See their partners in intimate relationships as alternately all good or all bad (splitting)

- Misread signals from others, overreacting to signals that threaten to stimulate old pain (alexthemia)

- Lose the ability to let go and be playful in intimate relationships (loss of ability to fantasize, symbolize)

- Lose the ability to trust and have faith in intimate relationships (interruption of affiliative bond)

- Lose their capacity to accept support (numbness, shutdown, unresolved pain)

- Engage in sensation-seeking behavior (high intensity/shutdown)

- Self-medicate with drugs and alcohol (self-medication)

The Effect of Trauma on the Fundamental Aspects of Relationships

People with unresolved trauma and grief issues carry their repressed pain and distorted perceptions and beliefs into adult intimate relationships. This can complicate adult relationships in some of the following areas.

Intimacy: The intense feelings of dependency, love and fear that are aroused in an intimate relationship can make a trauma survivor feel both deeply connected and deeply anxious. Because trauma interrupts the affiliative bond and trauma and loss survivors have experienced deep hurt and disillusionment in significant relationships, when they reattach later in life, it can feel perilous and frightening. This very response, however, can lead to healing because issues that need to be worked through and repressed feelings that need to be felt in order to heal are brought to the surface. Taking the risk of being in an intimate relationship also provides an opportunity for healing and growth.

Commitment: Commitment brings up fear for the person who has loved and lost or been abused or wounded in the area of intimate relationships. Unconsciously, the person who has experienced deep wounding and interruption of a primary attachment bond fears making another deep attachment. Trauma survivors carry deep fears alternately of abandonment or engulfment. These are two extremes, two sides of the same coin, and a person might adopt one of them or alternate between the two. In any case, these fears can keep the survivors in a state of anxiety around the subject of commitment. They may act them out either by rashly rushing into commitment without giving themselves time to get to know a person, or by becoming commitment-phobic, trying to stay clear of anything that feels permanent. Trauma survivors or people who carry unresolved grief may also secretly blame themselves for what they consider the failure of a previous attachment. Though they were not necessarily at fault, they may still carry the distorted perception that they were at fault, that they are fundamentally incapable of intimacy. Though this

©1997 Tian Dayton, *Heartwounds*

may not be a conscious fear, it can lay buried in the unconscious and make survivors fearful of commitment.

Communication: Communication is a subtle give-and-take. It includes picking up on the signals between people, reading them reasonably accurately, and acting and reacting based on information interpreted from them. It is also direct and requires the ability to tune in on our own internal state, understand it and put it into words; to use language to accurately symbolize or represent emotional or psychological states; then to communicate, through appropriate language, those states to another person. Next, it is listening with an open mind to another person's description of his or her inner experience—listening without overreacting, labeling or getting triggered in such a way that communication stops. This type of communication requires skills that are unfortunately often undermined by trauma. Trauma undermines the accurate reading of subtle signals and distorts interpretations that can become fixed and inflexible in the mind of the trauma survivor. It disorganizes and shuts down access to the survivor's inner world, leaving a person with repressed wounds that get easily triggered and get in the way of building healthy boundaries. It is no wonder, then, that communication in intimate relationships is greatly impaired for those who carry unresolved grief and trauma wounds. Some of the work in relationships is couple's work and some needs to be attended to by each individual, then brought back to the couple. Communication in a couple caught in a cycle of reenactments can easily become a repository for unexpressed aggression; thus "talking things over" does not necessarily lead to resolution for this couple, as it turns into a subtler form of reliving and relieving aggression toward each other.

Boundaries: Another problem for trauma survivors in relationships is the desire to fuse or isolate as a way of attaching to another person. Healthy relationships are characterized by an ability to move in and out of co-states. A relationship consists of two personal states and a co-state that is, the state of each individual, then the two together. Fusion disallows this co-state in which each person is allowed to be in the presence of another while maintaining a sense of self. Isolation is the other side of fusion and is also a way of avoiding the co-state. Boundaries require that each person maintain a sense of self while in relationship with the other in a way that is flexible enough so that each person gets what he or she needs, not necessarily every moment, but in the overall picture.

In trauma, the inner object world of survivors becomes disorganized and distorted. Feelings—such as love and aggression, isolation and safety—get fused. People come to distorted conclusions about why things happen. They may think: "I get hurt when I am sad, I get rejected when I share my true feelings." Then they live by those distortions, assiduously avoiding situations that they fear may trigger pain. This undermines their sense of safety within themselves, and they see safety as being secured by anticipating and manipulating what other people might do. Without a secure sense of self based on an undistorted inner world, it is difficult to have healthy boundaries, because in order to have healthy boundaries, we must have a reasonably secure grasp on our own inner world and our own inner truth.

Modulating emotion: Trauma survivors learn to alternate between high-intensity feeling states and emotional shutdown; they do not learn to modulate their emotions by titrating the amount of emotion appropriate for a given situation. Instead, they may leap from 1 to 10 in their emotional response, whether or not this volume of emotion fits the situation. Their traumatized history has, in effect, taught them that emotional responses are all or nothing, and they continue this pattern throughout their lives. The ability to modulate emotion is central to any healthy relationship, as is the ability to listen without either withdrawing or blowing up, or to explain one's self in a manner that is useful and descriptive rather than blaming or disowning. Feeling strong emotion without shutting down or acting rashly allows intimacy to grow, as it provides the space for two people to work through emotionally laden conflicts without fleeing. When the powerful feelings that are a natural part of intimacy come, they can overwhelm the trauma survivors, who may then engage the fight, flight, freeze response. Learning to modulate these emotions by sitting through them, feeling their power and attempting to communicate what is being felt, promotes intimacy and a sense of safety. This is part of the process of recovery from trauma.

Trust and faith: Trauma interrupts or assaults the affiliative bond, or the intimate bond that connects people to one another. When that bond is undermined to the extent that it no longer performs its function of creating a pathway for connection, learning, security and communication, the result is a loss of trust and faith. Later, adult trauma survivors hesitate to form new deep attachments because they unconsciously fear that the bond will prove traumatizing or disappointing. Trust and faith are necessary for any deep and lasting relationship to succeed. No relationship is without its problems, and trust and faith are needed in order to summon the good will necessary to work through conflicts, and to understand that staying with a relationship and resolving problems will be worth it in the long run for all concerned. We do not always know the answers in working with intimate relationships, so faith in a higher good and trust in the benefits of relationships are necessary to create an atmosphere in which love can grow.

Accepting love and support: Traumatized people learn to shut down their inner world, to escape it through dissociation or to become adversarial. They lose their ability to take in support from the outside community. Relationships require give and take. Unfortunately, people are biologically programmed to learn how to accept love at particular developmental stages through kinship relationships. When the necessary nourishment is not forthcoming, a lifelong hunger develops, and survivors try to fill that hunger later in life, but they are left trying to fill it at the wrong time with the wrong people. Therapy creates a synthetic situation that allows regression to happen so that those hungers can surface and be filled with corrective experiences of nourishment and connection. Trauma survivors need to relearn how to accept love and support, how to let them in and be nourished by them. Intimate relationships that allow these hungers to be filled can help to heal the trauma survivor.

Having fun: People who have been traumatized can lose their ability to symbolize and fantasize, or they can develop an unconscious fear that fun will lead to a loss of control and chaos. We remember that some of the fallout of trauma is a loss of ability to take in support. Having fun requires an ability to let go of control, to enter a world in which fantasy can play a role, and generally to allow other people in with a spontaneous give and take. All of these abilities are undermined by the experience of trauma. For a person who has experienced a disaster, letting go might trigger fears of another disaster; for a person who has lived with alcoholism, fun may feel precarious, as if, in a split second, it could turn to chaos; and for those who have experienced a deep loss, fun may trigger pain from what was lost but not fully mourned. The ability to be spontaneous—that is, to respond appropriately and adequately in the moment—is a sign of mental health. Activities such as games and team sports, or therapies such as psychodrama and the creative arts therapies, help introduce and train this ability.

PART IV

Transformation and Healing Through Grief

Aloys Wach

Become willing
to take a leap of faith and
to risk trusting and having
faith in relationships.

Create self-care
time for nurturing.
Incorporate rewarding
activities and quiet
time into daily
schedule.

Examine how
the trauma is reenacted
in your present
relationship.

Negotiate time
together and
time on your
own.

Create a support
network and accept
support from
others.

Develop a
meaningful spiritual
life that helps you
feel centered,
anchored and in
touch with deeper
levels of life.

Incorporate
exercise and
good nutrition
into your
lifestyle.

Recognize an
wound or loss. S

Ask for
reassurance when
you need it.

Orig

Identify issues
around loss and trauma
and how they impact your
thinking, feeling and
behavior.

Recognize and
sit with powerful
feelings aroused by
intimacy and share
with partner in a
constructive manner
that promotes rather
than undermines intimacy.

Separate the
past from the present.
Is this problem current
or is it a vehicle for
expressing old,
unhealed pain?

Person

Create a new
narrative with new
insights and
meaning.

Effects

Personal Growth, In

# of Healing

Find personal meaning through personal pain, a personal philosophy of life.

Understand life lessons learned through adversity.

Learn to moderate compulsive behaviors so that they do not invade relationship space.

Feel feelings around loss or wound.

Identify transferences and projections that get lived out in your relationship.

Create time for the relationship —for activities that feel intimate, fun and meaningful.

Share the story and feelings with trusted people.

knowledge the nder to the pain.

Hurt

Sort out distorted perceptions about self and relationships that you have come to accept as true.

Share your inner life with partner where appropriate and constructive rather than withhold it.

Check things out with partner. Do reality checks around what you are feeling before accepting your interpretation as the only truth.

Changes

lationships

Learn to communicate deep feelings to partner and listen while partner communicates deep feelings to you.

ation and Resolution

rtwounds

Sadness flies on the wings of the morning and out
of the heart of darkness comes the light.

Jean Giraudoux, *The Madwoman of Chaillot*
Adapted by Maurice Valency

Grief should be the instructor of the wise;
Sorrow is Knowledge . . .

Lord Byron, *Manfried*

Where there is sorrow there is holy ground.

Oscar Wilde, *De Profundis*

Learn weeping and thou shalt gain laughing.

George Herberg, *Jacula Prudentum*

Transformation and Healing Through Grief

"A Deep Distress hath humanized my Soul . . ."

WILLIAM WORDSWORTH

In the Desert: The Way Out Is the Way Through

L ike fire, grief has the power to transform or destroy a person from within—to cleanse, purify and instruct the inner being or reduce it to ashes. The experience of grief humbles us, giving way to an awareness of the bare essentials of life, enhancing our awareness of what is truly important. Most of our personal problems come from running away rather than standing and facing pain. Paradoxically, the running away ultimately creates as many or more problems as those being avoided. If you looked into the lives of some of the world's greatest people, you would learn that more often than not their deepened energy, talent and commitment to the world have their origins in one or more experiences of working through and overcoming some major life problems. Great art and great thought are often the result of great suffering.

We have given suffering a bad name. In our feel-good society, we often see struggle as a sign of failure and may resent encountering our own personal trials and conflicts. But it is struggle, not the absence of it, that builds character, strength, self-esteem and personal power. Anyone who has made it through rather than run from adversity knows this. Mental health and spiritual health are deeply linked. Overcoming psychological and emotional blocks—grieving wounds, giving them a name and a process to heal them—cleanses and purifies the spirit and makes it ready to receive grace and wisdom. As the mind and emotional self grow, so does the spirit because they are woven of the same cloth. Grief, then, rather than a collapsing of the self, can be a surrendering to a process—the process of mourning.

Referring back to what I shared in the opening of this book, when I was able, as a teenager, to surrender to the pain and disillusionment of losing my father and my family as I knew it to addiction and divorce, I began the process of releasing myself from hurt, resentment and shame and opening myself to reconstructive experience. Then I could come to accept and integrate this loss and enter into the day-to-day process of rebuilding a new life. This has enabled me, over the years, not to shut the door on my past and the people in it but to reduce the central and powerful role that trauma might have played throughout my life. My family and I did the best we could, given what we had to bring to those struggles at the time, and that's as much as anyone can really do.

The Relationship Between Spirituality and Grief/Transformation

A grief experience pulls us away from our normal routines and accustomed frame of reference. It plunges us into an encounter with the self, creating an inner experience of such intensity that it cannot be ignored. It presses for a resolution and puts us in touch with the deeper experience of living. Any time this occurs there is an opportunity for personal growth. It is as if a fire burns away the excess material attached to the architecture of our inner world and we are forced to rebuild it—to look, save what is important and leave the rest behind in our attempt to survive. When life is reduced in this way, we are reduced as well. We see with stark clarity what is truly important, what we wish to hang onto and what we can let go. We become philosophers and see into the deeper meaning of life, love and the human experience. What is unimportant looks empty, even silly, while what we truly hold dear stands before us with a sort of luminescence. We are reborn into the very self, the very life we had discarded or lost or run from, and we deepen our capacity for intimacy. We awaken into another stage of living with a new hierarchy of values and meaning. We view the same landscape, but perceive it differently.

Intimate relationships provide one of the most basic and available paths for healing wounds to the heart. Trauma, remember, interrupts the attachment bond, causing a loss of trust and faith in life and in relationships. These wounds cannot be healed in isolation where they lay dormant—they need the re-creation of a relationship bond that stimulates them and brings them to the surface, where they can be seen and felt and healed. The painful feelings, when they come up, can feel unsurvivable, almost like an inner death, but the feelings that were repressed in order to allow us to survive can deaden our life force, keeping energy bound up and unavailable for the business of living.

Telling the Story: Bearing Witness

The process of healing from trauma and loss includes:

acknowledging the loss

telling the story and bearing witness to the pain

accepting support

linking current behavior with the original wound

separating the past from the present

creating a new narrative, placing the trauma story in the context of the overall life pattern with new insight

This process allows for energy to be freed up and reinvested. Telling our personal story gives the psyche an opportunity to integrate it into the personality. Great art, theater, poetry and song can be ways of sharing our story and having it witnessed. In psychodrama, we offer the clinical stage on which to "tell the story." A survivor will bring an internal issue that swims around his or her mind in a shapeless state into a concrete form by casting role players to represent the people involved in the conflict. It is a moment of time suspended in which a person can see what happened rather than turn away. In this way, the inner observer has an opportunity to view the contents of the mind that were shut down or out. It is profound and deeply moving to watch someone place his or her story, wounds, hurt, disappointment and disillusionment out into the supportive container of a group so that the person can have another chance to observe what is carried within. Simply doing this, feeling the emotions that come up and accepting support from the group, helps the trauma survivor who has lost access to his or her own insides.

In the following case study, we see that when James was able to be vulnerable, to acknowledge and experience his emotional response to his boss, rather than project the pain his employer was triggering in him onto his boss—as if the boss alone were the cause—James was able to gain some clarity about his painful relationship dynamics in his workplace.

James is a department head at a prominent university. He recently came to group fairly green with anticipation at the prospect of an upcoming retreat weekend with his boss and co-workers, and announced that he needed help. He put out an SOS to the group to do work. We set up the psychodrama. He wanted, in the safety of a clinical setting, to say what he needed to say to his boss so that it didn't come out inadvertently during the weekend. He set up two chairs and apologetically asked Jeff to play his boss. He began, "You're a snake in the grass, manipulative, you talk out of two sides of your mouth. I can't stand you. You don't have a clue how to manage people." Eventually it became evident to him that the feelings, if not all the words, matched those that he had toward his father. He chose someone to role-play his dad and the hurt underneath the anger surfaced. Tears choked his words as he asked, "Why couldn't you just love me, just want to be with me the way I was, because I was your son. Why did I have to work so hard for your love?"

James's boss only gave him positive feedback when he worked an 80-hour week. The more his boss expected, the harder James worked, stretching himself beyond anything that felt healthy or comfortable to him. As a young man, James was an excellent student, a talented athlete, super-responsible, and could only gain love and acceptance from his father when he was working beyond his comfort level—striving for perfection and validation, and even then it was never enough to please his dad. His boss's recent demand to put in extra time in order to be acceptable on the job triggered James's earlier unresolved conflict with his father. No wonder James feared the weekend.

He couldn't feel the difference on an emotional level between what was going on with his boss and what went on with his father. To complicate matters further, the retreat was being held at the boss's home. Thirty years earlier, James's father had kicked James out of his house the summer after his senior year for breaking the house rules. James never lived there again, going back for short stays only. Here he was again in a house of a man in charge. It felt too big, as if his boss were in charge not only of his job but of his life, and he felt like a 17-year-old boy all over again. Separating James's transference feelings—those belonging to the past—from the current situation gave James the ability to stand back and get a little perspective. He also reversed roles with his boss at one point, which gave him some insight into the feelings that might be inside of the boss. Then we built in reconstructive experiences by allowing him to replay the situation as he would have liked it to be. We gave him time to actually experience the feeling of being with his family in a way that would have felt good to him. This is the reconstructive portion of the drama that creates a new memory and introduces it into the person on a feeling, experiential level so that when old painful memories get triggered, the corrective memory will hopefully be there too.

The next week James shared that the weekend had been much better than he expected. He had said what he needed to say reasonably and without blaming and received much unexpected support both from co-workers and the group facilitator. As it turned out, he was not alone in finding his boss difficult, and through his work separating the boss from his feelings about his father he gained some emotional distance. Four months later, James's boss asked him to consult with him on managing the team who worked in the department, and he supported James in working a more reasonable set of hours.

Working with James on this issue was such a clear example to myself and the group members of how a complex, set up in childhood, gets played out over and over again until the transference or the old feelings that are being projected onto a new relationship get resolved. Once James "got it," he got out of his own way—the block was removed and he restored harmony almost immediately. He is an example of a client who can use therapy effectively. He is willing to look at himself and is motivated to incorporate behavioral changes once the emotions holding the problematic dynamic are made conscious.

After James worked through his transference toward his boss, he recognized that he lived this pattern out similarly in his intimate relationships. He overfunctioned to meet the demands of his partner without examining whether or not the demands were reasonable. Again, he put his dilemma onto the psychodramatic stage. This time he structured a scene with his girlfriend and his recently divorced wife of 27 years. One of the central aspects of the drama was a telephone. James was, you might say, hypervigilant around the subject of demands. He listened in frozen anticipation to the voices of his wife and girlfriend and read, within the first 30 seconds of hearing their voices, what they might want of him. At this point, he either shut down and withdrew or went into overdrive trying to accommodate or meet their expectations. He dreaded the very ring of his phone, which emerged as a metaphor of both his wish to connect and his fear of being close. "Close" had come to mean swinging into action to meet other people's expectations, allowing them to define the nature of the relationship rather than both of them negotiating it. When meeting expectations felt like too much, he saw the solution to his feeling of engulfment as a withdrawal into himself or out of the relationship. When James could examine and experience the feelings underneath, he saw his pattern in a new light, making connections as to its origin and identifying the ways in which it got repeated in his relationships. Once he understood it, he was able to change it—first by identifying it, next by making connections to the source and sharing his feelings rather than shutting down, and last by changing his behavior in ways that felt better to him and to his partner, thus promoting rather than undermining intimacy.

Another important aspect of James's healing was to go back to his early years and look for strength. In his case, that strength came from remembering his relationship with his father at an earlier time in his life, when it felt more comforting and supportive, before the intense expectations and pressures took over. He also identified other sources of support that were in his life, such as his mother and his sister, from whom he felt a more unconditional love, and the parents of his friends with whom he spent a great deal of time and who were kind to him and served as models for a more supportive type of relationship. I often ask clients to get in touch not only with their pain but also with their gifts and strengths and the sources of support from which they drew sustenance. James had the sort of personality that drew mentors and friends toward him, which gave him a certain resilience in overcoming his problems at home.

Therapy is a process of dismantling and rebuilding. It is important to focus on the positive alongside the painful, to engage with hope and faith as part of the curative process; to reawaken to the beauty life can offer and, where possible, develop a spiritual attitude toward living. Clients who have faith in God or some form of Higher Power often seem not only to heal faster but to hold the healing and put it into practice more successfully. They are able to connect with a broader life purpose and plan, which helps put trauma into a larger context and give it a meaning in the process of growing into a more spiritual person. They are also willing to open to the healing power of grace. When spiritual energy enters the room, laughter, joy, humanity and compassion enter along with it—simply put, the air itself changes. I have witnessed this happening so many times that I now accept the healing power of spirituality and see its role in resolving and integrating wounds to the heart as a profoundly useful and important part of the healing process.

Finding Meaning

Like the Zen monk, for whom enlightenment represents a change in seeing or a perceptual shift, the meaning found from trauma is a similar process of using life circumstances as grist for the mill of soulmaking. For the student of Zen, meaning does not lead to enlightenment if it is simply a rhetorical spewing out of someone else's thoughts on the subject; personal growth comes only through using the events and circumstances, however mundane, of one's *own* life. The meaning that leads toward spiritual enlightenment has to be come upon by the deep and rocky search of our own path, diving deep into the lake of the personal unconscious and examining its contents. This is the key to unlocking the door that will reveal profound truth. We have only the vehicle of self to work through. Overcoming painful life circumstances does not mean that we beat our world into an orderly submission. Rather, it means that through encounter and examination of our own, inner world we learn to see life as an expression of spirit—always talking to us, always revealing its lessons one layer at a time.

The meaning that comes from struggle and pain is our own, it belongs uniquely to us. No one can give it to us and once seen, no one can take it away. It is what allows us to rise above circumstances of life and see them in a way that returns us to a sense of inner peace. This is why we seek meaning: to restore balance and tranquility, to return life to a state in which we see it differently, to read it in such a way as to allow us to live it with some degree of understanding and equanimity.

The New Narrative: Retelling the Story, Constructing New Meaning

One of the final stages of healing from the trauma of loss lies in finding meaning through struggle and pain. This process of inner searching is what separates humans from beasts—it is our human ability to learn from and find meaning in life events, to grow and evolve through pain and struggle. Seeing what happened long ago through the eyes of the present, we will first reexperience it as we experienced it then. If it is a painful memory, this is the hard part, where we will be tempted to shut down or re-repress the memory. But if we can sit through it and witness it in the here and now, we become conscious of what we were unconscious of before. We find it alters before our inner vision because we are viewing it afresh through adult eyes.

As previously discussed, reconstructing is the process of *doing, undoing* and *redoing*. First we do or feel as we did then; we reexperience the memory as we experienced it then. Next we undo and examine or deconstruct the meaning that we originally assigned to our early experience. Then we redo; we reconstruct the original situation with new awareness, insight and meaning. This allows for new, healthier learning experiences to be introduced into the symbolic re-creation of a trauma so that when the memory is recalled later, not only the pain but the healing will surface also. Introducing and creating reconstructive memories is a crucial part of the healing process so that a person does not cycle endlessly through pain. Catharsis of pain is only part of the healing. If we constantly process pain without introducing new nourishing experiences, we start, as Albert Pesso of Psychomotor Mind-Body Therapy says, "to eat the pain instead of the satisfaction because the nourishment isn't being given." He goes on to say that the "reconstructive memory needs to be kinesthetic," or experienced by the body and mind together. The brain learns by doing. According to the brain, to do is to know. The corrective experience needs to be experienced with full engagement of the mind, emotions and body in order for the brain to learn it fully. People find meaning each in their own way. Revelation comes from without as well as from within.

In her own words, Maya tells her story of working through pain and opening to new experience. Maya was a classic parentified child. When her family moved from Mexico to the U.S., her mother had a nervous breakdown and Maya took over the role of parenting her younger siblings and being her mother's support and confidante. This position made it difficult for her to individuate and become her own person during her teenage and adult years. Consequently, she has had trouble moving forward in her own profession and claiming her own life. A professional writer, she expresses this quiet drama in her own words with touching clarity.

My mother had an overwhelming need for me to not separate from her, to remain as close as possible to her idealized image of who she would wish herself and me to be. I was thus deprived of the opportunity to fully explore my identity, to become separate and different, to learn how to express my own voice and style and wants and needs. While my friends battled their mothers during adolescence, acting out in ways big and small, I colluded with my mother in maintaining what we both proudly perceived to be our "close relationship." I never questioned why I couldn't wait each June to leave home for eight weeks and return to Mexico, where I worked at a summer school. For 10 months of the year, I was depressed and filled with self-hatred; I rated myself the "third-ugliest girl" in the high school I attended. Only during the summer months, free of and far away from Mother, did I feel magically transformed into a person who felt happy and pretty and sexually attractive—a person worth knowing. But I never made the connection, never rebelled.

I dutifully marched down the path that I unconsciously understood she chose for me to follow. I went to the college she wanted me to go to (because she would have wanted to study at such a college); broke up with someone I loved (and dreamed about for years afterwards) because she didn't approve of him;

married the boy-man she would have handpicked for me had I given her the chance; chose the safe profession of teacher because I was supposed to work at a nice little job until I started having babies, just as she had done.

When my life felt as if it were crashing in around me and I went into therapy, she angrily asked, "Why do *you* need therapy?" She'd given me the perfect childhood—so she thought—meant to redeem all the suffering she'd endured as a child. I couldn't possibly be unhappy or have anything to complain about to a therapist. But I had plenty to talk about, years worth of despair and depression. I started grasping slivers of the truth about how my mother had used me to try to satisfy her own insatiable needs. She had never healed her childhood wounds; now I was trying to recover from the wounds she'd unwittingly inflicted on me.

Over time, my carefully nurtured illusions about myself, my parents and my family were stripped away. What I didn't realize was that beneath the many layers of denial and repression lay a huge, deep pool of rage into which I only occasionally allowed myself to peer. But I was too frightened to truly examine its depths, and for the most part I danced around the rim, not daring to immerse myself—until eventually I almost drowned.

A work crisis—a book I couldn't write—triggered a massive depression. I felt angry and bitter, and my mother was the primary target of those feelings. At my insistence, we didn't speak for most of the year, and then we began an excruciating series of counseling sessions. Finally, I allowed myself to release the long-buried rage that had been boiling at my core. I literally exploded, hating her so fully that I often couldn't stay seated as I screamed and bellowed and ranted at her. I was, at last, starting to become separate, my own person. I felt raw and exposed, bewildered and unmoored. In order to heal, I had to pull back, examine who I was, explore who I wanted to be.

Soon, perhaps inevitably, my grief and rage spilled over onto my partner. For a time I needed also to separate from him. I had to be alone, so that finally, I had the space to attend only to myself. I discovered new pleasures in my day-to-day life, in making my own decisions, allowing myself small indulgences without having to consider anyone else's needs. And in psychodrama, I worked at further releasing my rage, mourning my grief, healing. Five years later, I still recall a moment of understanding that was the closest I've ever come to a spiritual epiphany. I could not move forward until I could forgive. And in forgiving, I also had to apologize for the hurts I'd caused my partner, my mother and a close friend with whom I'd had a terrible falling-out. "I'm sorry" had never come easily to me. Now I had to make—chose to make—not one, but three very difficult and heartfelt apologies.

I forgave and asked forgiveness. In doing so, I started opening my heart, moment by moment, to being more compassionate, less judgmental, more loving and accepting of my weaknesses, and the weaknesses of the people I love. I have come to understand that spiritual growth—which I define as a growth of my spirit, and a deepening belief in the wondrous possibilities that the universe offers us—is very much an ongoing process. I continue to peel away the layers of grief that still lie within me. I continue to flounder as I arrive at yet another frontier of sadness and self-awareness. "What?" I cry. "I'm here again?"

Recently, I find that I am grieving anew for my child self. I am mourning the choices—good and bad—that I could have made, the missed joys and terrors I could have given myself. I am mourning the opportunities and experiences that were lost to me because my inner voice wasn't strong enough to call my attention to them. I am mourning the books I haven't written, the babies I haven't given birth to, because my inner voice, my child self, is still so fragile, still too tightly bound to my mother's vision of who I am. I fight to break those bonds, to continue to create my own definition of self. And I struggle to sustain a spirited and spiritually healthy relationship with that self . . . whoever she/I may be.

After Maya was able to better understand the origins of her problems, she began to see how and when they got projected onto her partner. This enabled her not only to actually marry him, but also to talk through rather than act out her buried pain. She could use her relationship with her husband as a vehicle for growth and restoration. She and her husband now have an unusually supportive and deep partnership. On a daily basis she reaps the rewards of her work in the beautiful connection she shares with her life partner.

We construct our personal meaning from our experience of the life events in which we find ourselves. Our construction of meaning has a large subjective element—that is, it is based on the way we *see* an event at a point in time. How we see an event is different from how it is seen by another person. How we interpret and give meaning to a situation depends on a number of factors such as the size and level of our vulnerability in a situation, our emotional and/or physical development up to that time, our self-image, our interpersonal skills and our own personal delegation of symbolic meaning; all that goes into our personal history.

Research on eyewitness accounts radically altered our ideas about how the same event or circumstance can be—and indeed is—viewed wholly differently by each person witnessing it. Interpretation is in the eye of the beholder. Life is a series of events and circumstances to which we assign our own meaning. We view our lives through our own particular lens; we interpret and construct meaning based on who we are, what we have learned and how we have learned it up until that point. In creating a new narrative, we first examine and come to understand how we have constructed our own system of personal meaning. We then deconstruct that meaning, we take it apart, look at it, wonder about it and come to new insights about how we experienced our own life. This process in and of itself will alter meaning because when we look at past events and interpret them through our eyes of today, we see them differently, with new understanding, compassion and insight. We will understand not only the how but the why—why it is that we interpreted a circumstance in a particular way at a particular time, and why it meant what it meant then, even though we might see it differently today. We reframe our life events. We reconstruct our assignation of personal meaning, weaving through our newly constructed story the revelations and new insight that we have gained through careful observation and reexperiencing of our own inner world. It is, in a sense, the same story told differently, with new insight and understanding, seen from a new perspective. As Judith Herman so clearly puts it:

> Out of the fragmented components of frozen imagery and sensation, patient and therapist slowly reassemble an organized, detailed, verbal account oriented in time and historical context. The narrative includes not only the event itself but also the survivor's response to it and the responses of the important people in her life. As the narrative closes in on the most unbearable moments, the patient finds it more and more difficult to use words. At times the patient may spontaneously switch to nonverbal methods of communication, such as drawing or painting. Given the "iconic," visual nature of traumatic memories, creating pictures may represent the most effective initial approach to these "indelible images." Reconstructing of the trauma story begins with a review of the patient's life before the trauma and the circumstances that led up to the event. Yael Danieli speaks of the importance of reclaiming the patient's earlier history in order to "re-create the flow" of the patient's life and restore a sense of continuity with the past. The patient should be encouraged to talk about her important relationships, her ideals and dreams, and her struggles and conflicts prior to the traumatic event. This exploration provides a context within which the particular meaning of the trauma can be understood (Herman, 1992, p. 177).

The Spiritual Solution: An Angle of Vision

After you resolve and integrate a trauma and pass through a process of mourning, an important portion of the solution to living well with loss becomes a spiritual one that embraces the deeper mysteries of life. The key to dealing well with loss, to allowing it to be a growth experience, turning it into another kind of gain, requires a shift in perspective. Emerson called life an "angle of vision." The same life can look many different ways depending upon *how* we are viewing it, depending upon *our* angle of vision. Viktor Frankl credits attitude for his ability to survive Nazi concentration camps with his spirit not only intact but stronger. He discovered the one singular thing that his captors could not take from him was his attitude. It is in part attitude—each individual's angle of vision—that allows some people to grow from loss while others are beaten by it. While this is not the only factor, it is much larger than anyone admits. Ask those who have succeeded in overcoming obstacles and moving forward into life in positive ways, and they will often tell you that their attitude and faith are what lie behind their success.

Life inevitably contains loss. One thing we can count on is that life will be difficult and disappointing at times. It is not the fact of life's disillusionment and disappointment, but how we *see* it that can make the difference between using problems to grow from or feeling defeated by life. The following are attitude adjustments that help trauma survivors face loss from a spiritual perspective.

(1) *Helplessness* is shifted into *powerlessness.* People who have been traumatized feel helpless. They could do nothing to affect, change or stop something bad from happening, whether that something was a flood or being neglected by a parent. A person who goes through life feeling helplessness can adopt this as a life position of "learned helplessness." They can translate that into thinking that there is no point in trying—that trying won't help

anyway. Moving from helplessness to powerlessness is just a shift in perception, but one that allows for a move from victimization to empowerment. A chosen recognition of powerlessness allows a person to cease trying to control and manipulate events. It recognizes that we are powerless over certain life events, that we cannot protect ourselves from some pain, and that when pain comes it's not necessarily because we were bad, inadequate or wrong—life was not aiming at us. The truth is simply that part of life is pain that no one can avoid. In fact, to go through life trying to avoid it is pathology-making. Much of pathological behavior—drug and alcohol abuse, sexual abuse and so on—is an attempt to assuage the experience of personal pain, to medicate it. The assumption beneath is that life should not be painful—we do not want it to be, and when it is we try to disown it because feeling it makes us feel too vulnerable. Feeling vulnerable and helpless can lead to anger, frustration, disillusionment and a host of additional painful feelings. Then we try to manage the pain rather than feel it, to avoid it rather than allow it, to reject and judge it rather than learn from it. Misguided attempts to manage pain make pain a sort of master within the psyche, giving it enormous power to make us run from our selves and hide from our own minds and hearts.

(2) *Hypervigilance* is shifted into *surrender*. Expecting loss and understanding that life will inevitably disappoint at times allows us to shift away from hypervigilance toward surrender. Hypervigilance is a rigid position, a taut branch that cannot bend in the wind, a position that leaves a person at the mercy of the forces of nature, fighting against them, trying to manage and change them. Surrender allows for the forces of nature, a branch that *can* bend in the wind; pliable, supple, able to bend without breaking. Surrendering to pain is what allows a person to grow from it. By experiencing pain, it deepens a connection with self; it purifies what the yogis call the lower self. All major

religions speak of cleansing the lower self in order to prepare the vehicle of a higher self for contact with a Higher Power. The grief process is a time-honored path of purification, the intrapsychic catharsis of the aesthetic.

(3) *Isolation* shifts into *building a support network*, a *restoration of attachment bonds*. People who have been traumatized through some type of loss withdraw into themselves and lose their ability to access community support. *Reaching out and asking for help* changes this dynamic of continued isolation to one of actually building a support network. Implicit in this network building is the repairing of attachment or affiliative bonds. Trauma at its very core disorganizes the inner world of the survivor. It interrupts, rearranges and otherwise undermines what the survivor has accepted as real and true. Feelings within the inner world get fused together like wires in an electrical short or fire. Violence and love may become fused pain and ambition ("I'm only doing this because I love you." "This is for your own good."), as well as sexuality, aggression and secrecy ("Let me touch you, gratify myself, don't complain, don't whimper and don't tell."). Crazy-making, conflicting meanings got soldered together in the brain, and when survivors reach out for love in the future, they cannot accept or recognize love that does not come with these other meanings attached to it. Consequently, survivors unconsciously choose that very situation they wish to avoid. It is part of the legacy of trauma.

Examine the painful repeated choices and actions in your life to understand which particular experiences you found traumatizing. It's an old story that children of alcoholics unwittingly choose other children of alcoholics or alcoholic partners in marriage. All of the covert emotions and behaviors attached to the alcoholic or the child of an alcoholic are welded together in the brain with intimacy, love, home and family, so the brain recognizes the pattern it has previously bonded with and incorporated into the self and bonds with it again. The isolation of trauma can be partially treated through creating a support network. Trauma inhibits our ability to take in support; a consistent support network acts as an antidote to correct this problem.

(4) *Loss of trust and faith* reaches toward the spiritual solution of *anchoring to a faith in God or a Higher Power.* Trauma, as we have discussed earlier in the book, produces a loss of trust and faith. The relationships that we depended upon were profoundly disappointing, which made us lose faith in the relationship bond. This type of deep disappointment can lead to a bottoming out where the survivor of trauma loses faith not only in relationships to others but also in relationships with self and life. It is, in a sense, a spiritual crisis that begs for a spiritual solution. The confusion, disappointment and disillusionment attendant upon bottoming out leave a survivor feeling an existential despair. But out of this despair, hope can come. It is deeply strengthening to go through pain and struggle and to survive, to know that you can surmount life's difficulties. It is at these moments of despair that we meet God and self, that we go within and look for strength, that we learn to trust ourselves, and through that relationship with self that we recognize God's presence within us. My grandmother used to say that the only real faith is blind faith—faith not in what we see but in what we become willing to see and embrace. This deepens a relationship with self and God and leads to a self-confidence based on an inner knowledge that we can survive pain and allow life to restore and rebuild itself. The more of life we can embrace, the more spiritual our lives can become.

In fact, recognizing spirit in all things transforms our experience of life and the world we live in. In his book *Finding God on a Train: A Journey into Prayer,* Rick Hamline remembers how his father demonstrated this embracing attitude in evening prayers.

For instance, when my little sister and I started giggling he [my father] asked God to bless our high spirits and good humor. When the German shepherd next door started to bark at some distant siren, he thanked God for the dog. . . . What to do with the interruptions in prayer? Include them, for goodness sake. Maybe they are God's way of reminding us to add something or someone to our prayer list. . . . Next time you pray or meditate, notice what distracts you. Rather than ignoring these interruptions, embrace them, giving thanks for how they have enriched your life (Hamline, 1997).

Reorganizing a Memory

One could see neurotic, compulsive, co-dependent or addictive behavior as an attempt to find a solution from the outside world to solve a problem in our inner world, using normal behavior in an abnormal way. Work, hyperactivity or substances such as food, drugs or alcohol can be used in an unconscious attempt to bring calm to inner chaos. Feelings need to be felt to be understood and integrated into the self-system.

Grief comes from somewhere. A memory is stored in a cell assembly in the brain, and when that cell assembly rises to the surface in the conscious mind, it can be looked at by the inner observer or that part of the mind that has the ability to witness its own mental process. This simple act of observing will be very informative if we learn to watch and feel rather than dismiss and act. We are grieving the loss of something or someone that was meaningful to us. The loss was to some extent painful or traumatizing. Any one of the responses to trauma that we discussed earlier of fight, flight or freeze precludes the full processing of emotional pain. The function of these responses is to ensure survival, to allow us to protect ourselves from immediate physical or emotional pain. They work for the moment; they allow us to continue to function, but eventually we will need to feel and process these feelings that we put "on hold." If we do not feel them, they do not disappear—the "unfelt known" will seek relief. It may be projected onto another person, and we will see their anger but not our own. We may overreact, becoming irrationally angry, in order to relieve our own built-up anger, or we may shut down and withdraw.

When we understand what is going on within us, we alter the cell assembly in the brain. Learning is a process of paring down and building up brain cells. When we experience a memory *consciously* we reorganize the memory; we have the opportunity to see it in a new light, discarding what no longer fits and adding new insight. And when we reintegrate the assembly or the memory back into the unconscious, it is relieved of some of its power. It is filed correctly instead of repressed. It is not only the memory itself that is the problem but what we *do* with the memory within ourselves because of the meaning that it carries for us. This could also be seen as a sort of reframing. We learn to *see* the memory differently, which means that it will have a different effect on us.

Another way in which unresolved grief can fuel dysfunctional behavior is as an acting-out of buried shame. Pain can make us feel isolated, different from other people. Loss can cause us to pull back from life, feeling as if we are watching our life rather than living it. When shame becomes too painful to carry in banished inner silence, it may seek relief through some form of self-medication. Any behavior or substance that provides momentary relief can be a panacea, the "answer" to our dilemma. If some liquor or food or activity felt good, more will be better—and so the cycle of addiction begins. The more the solution is seen as lying outside the self, the weaker the self becomes. I work with these types of addictions daily. There are an estimated 138 million people in the United States whose lives are involved with substance addiction. The link between unresolved trauma and substance abuse is clear, evidenced in the trauma victim's desire to self-medicate.

Here is Judy's story. A recovering alcoholic, she entered therapy in order to resolve the issues that she previously medicated with drugs and alcohol.

A hip, downtown type of woman, an art teacher who dressed in a tasteful, offbeat manner, Judy had a great exterior—though as our sessions progressed it was increasingly evident that she had a very weak connection with her inner world. She chose, each week, to sit in a chair that allowed her to sink back, to remove herself slightly from the intensity of the group. Invariably, when other group members were doing painful work around feelings of loss, Judy felt a need to get a drink of water or go to the ladies' room. She made no connection between the nature of the work and her impulse to leave. My first task with Judy was to develop a bond with her, one that could help her to hold feelings that she herself hardly knew she had. Her own strong emotions rendered her inarticulate. She cried a lot but she seldom knew why. She was unable to identify what she was feeling when she cried or got angry, which left her reacting strongly but having little sense of what triggered her reaction. Fortunately for both of us, I thoroughly liked her. Her great sense of humor and good-heartedness, her style, her need of warmth and acceptance drew me toward her. She could find humor in anything, a skill that had given her an important role in her family—she had been useful to them because she diverted worry and concern onto herself. She was a classic mascot who relieved tension for her family, but this role evolved into that of a scapegoat in that her family eventually came to identify her as the "problem."

One theme emerged over the weeks. Occasionally, I found myself feeling very loving feelings toward Judy. Invariably, when I was feeling particularly affectionate, she asked me if I was mad at her or she said, "I'm afraid you hate me." At first this baffled me (and the group), but the pattern became so consistent that I came to understand that she associated love with rejection. I surmised that she had not been able to accommodate and integrate her paradoxical feelings of love and hate toward a parent without fear of losing the relationship. Love and hate are natural feelings on the part of any child. Children need to learn that they can feel both feelings without destroying the relationship. In the confused emotional container of Judy's family, where her role had been to act out everyone else's pain, she had little time to feel or understand her own. When she sensed pain she swung into action, cracking a joke, leaving the room—anything to put a lid on the anxiety it stirred.

Each time Judy was confronted with a life loss, it returned her to a state of childhood fear. Intimacy in any relationship includes loving and losing on a daily basis, negotiating the vicissitudes of closeness and distance, trusting that neither will last forever and that both will happen over and over again. For Judy, closeness triggered anxiety, her fear of distance, her fear of rejection. Her response was that her inner world would do a sort of flip. She would move from feeling safe to terrified in less than a minute. She had, in her repertoire, a thousand ways of distancing people. It was her childlike way of protecting herself. When she did get close, it gave rise to critical and angry feelings toward the person she was close to, which eventually gave way to angry outbursts, hurt feelings and distance once again. Because Judy had not had a parent who could tolerate her powerful feelings and needs, she was left yearning and searching for a feeling of closeness that, when she attained it, made her feel anxious and frightened. She could not take it for granted that if someone liked her, the person would continue to like her. Instead, that very liking made her brace for rejection and eventually participate in creating it.

Once Judy felt the pain of being the identified "problem child" and the fear and anxiety it created in her, she engaged in the work of building the self that she had been denying. She had learned to dismiss her real feelings as an adult in the same way she had been dismissed as a child. Suddenly she would lose touch with her sense of safety and connectedness. The people around her, in this case myself and the group, would shift from feeling safe to feeling threatening, from feeling close and supportive to distant and detached, and she was unable at those times to find her way back from alienation to reconnection. At this point, she would dig a sort of hole for herself, acting in ways that further alienated her from those around her. Judy needed help identifying what was getting triggered for her at those times. This required her to learn to sit with her painful feelings rather than venting them through outbursts of anger and blame. As the scapegoat, Judy had come to see herself as somehow defective, which made her feel like defending herself. She carried a great deal of shame around being seen in this way and felt hurt and rejected by her family, whom she loved and wanted acceptance from. The more they rejected her, the more she acted out. What Judy didn't realize is that she was, in a sense, acting out unresolved pain for the whole family. Once she understood this, some of the shame lifted and she was able to separate herself from her role. Some of the responsibility for any given problem was, naturally, hers—but certainly not all of it. When she let go of being the container for her family pain, she began rebuilding her own identity, and taking responsibility for her behavior became less threatening.

Judy's progress has been somewhat remarkable. She eventually ended a relationship that constantly re-created her scapegoat role and is now engaged to a man with whom she has a healthy relationship dynamic. When she gets triggered and acts out now, she can identify her pattern and talk about it so that a crisis that previously occurred over and over again is intervened on now within one or two days. She has demystified her inner world and can talk about her intense feelings and identify them with impressive clarity. Judy's joy in living and her ability to both feel it within herself and share it with others has become nothing short of a gift to those around her. Her commitment to therapy has paid off. Slowly over time, the self that hid in fear and needed protection has emerged, and her inner witness has strengthened so that the feelings she used to run from now allow her to better know who she is.

To Thine Own Self Be True: How the Grief Process Allows Us to Move On in Life

Learning from loss happens on an emotional, cognitive and spiritual level. An emotional feeling, much like a physical feeling, tells us where and how much something hurts. When we do not feel our feelings, we lose this source of information. Ungrieved wounds ask us to operate at a serious deficit. Being up-to-date by processing feeling on a daily basis enhances our ability to walk through life with more of ourselves available to respond. On a spiritual level, letting go is part of how we learn. We open to the gifts that we earn through deep and painful psychological and emotional experience . . . through trial by fire. Trial seems to be a part of most spiritual teaching. Spiritual knowledge has the paradoxical quality of being sought but not found. Instead, it comes as a result of deep experience—it is won on the altar of life.

Using life circumstances to grow from, rather than as an excuse to throw in the towel and stop trying, is the thesis of this book. There is an Italian saying: *Even fruit is bitter before it is ripe.* The feeling of bitterness is a natural part of development and inner struggle. We may often say to ourselves: Why me? Life isn't on my side, this isn't fair. Who is not prey to these feelings of angst? But remaining in bitterness and despair means we never ripen as a person, never allow growth to happen. Painful circumstances are fertilizer spread over the field of self, giving way to new growth: The self becomes stronger and healthier for having been tilled and fertilized.

Judy needed to experience her bitterness and hurt before she could allow love into her life. Once her reservoir of pain lessened, she was less likely to blindly react to the daily problems in her relationship. Until the pain was drained, each little hurt threw her back into her hidden past, which made the current daily problem feel huge and unsolvable. Through therapy she was able to move through a process of grief and learn from rather than continually play out or re-create old pain.

Our humanity does not spring full-grown. Instead, it is earned through the contests and challenges of daily life, pounded and chiseled on the blacksmith's white-hot furnace. No one escapes pain—avoiding it forces us to avoid portions of our own inner world and aspects of the outer world. Facing grief gives the self the freedom it needs to breathe, and that breath is necessary to sustain life. We cannot cut off grief without amputating portions of the self, without silencing our own inner voice.

What blocks a person from being able to grieve? Grief can become blocked when (1) we get stuck in a particular phase of the grief cycle; (2) conditions in the environment do not support our expression of the painful emotions of mourning; (3) the conflicts with a lost person or circumstance are too intense to be faced openly; or (4) a parent negatively influences a child's grief process. Freud explained grief work as the disinvestment of energy in memories of the lost person, place or circumstances. We can see how grief gets revived throughout the life cycle by identifying certain triggers. The same processes underlie both normal and disordered mourning. Grief and trauma wounds begin to be resolved when we surrender to the power and depth of our own feelings, and we open a door to self. When we close the door on grief, we say no to the entry of significant pieces of self. When survivors can direct their attention toward the trauma or away from it at will—that is, when they can think about the trauma and then turn their mind toward other subjects through their own choice—healing has occurred.

In a form of grief work, many great artists create from their own brokenness—the drive toward art and creation springs from the need to give voice to this brokenness, bringing it out from the deepest reaches of our inner world into the light of day. Art has the ability to concretize inner experience, to give shape to that which floats around the psyche in a shapeless state. It portrays inner experience not only as it is seen in the world, but as it is seen in the mind's eye, combining word and symbol so they make sense to the heart. This great form of human expression is born of a willingness to grapple and struggle with personal dilemmas; it is a human solution to a human problem. First, it attempts to communicate with the deepest portions of the self (the personal), then it brings a new language through which to communicate with another (interpersonal). These are artistic solutions to integrate loss and grief, and each and every one of us has the potential to access this artist who lives within us, who can help us make sense and meaning out of what feels senseless and meaningless.

Grief and the Birth of the Artist

Not everyone talks their way through grief. Deep emotional pain can be symbolized in creative language, channeling hurt, anger and aggression into a work of creative expression. The grief experience can awaken the inner artist. The artist self comes to the aid of the suffering self by giving that part of us a voice in which to express the pain of mourning. Painting, journaling, song and dance can give symbol and voice to inner wounds that cannot speak in words. Two poignant examples of this are the artist Kathe Kollowitz and the author Rudyard Kipling. George H. Pollock, M.D., Ph.D., speaks of Kathe Kollowitz, whose mother was never able to resolve the grief of losing her young son, Kathe's brother. Children make meaning out of loss that parents may be wholly unaware of:

> . . . memories of Benjamin's illness and death were deeply stamped on Kathe's mind. As a mature woman and even in her old age she recalled how she had ached with love and pity as a reserved mother had grieved silently for Benjamin. . . . Kathe was tormented by feelings of guilt because of a strange circumstance that occurred at the time of Benjamin's death. [Their] father had wanted his children to have worthwhile playthings and had given them large building blocks . . . from these Kathe had built for her own use a temple to Venus . . . she was playing at worship in this temple when her mother and father, quietly coming into the room, had told her that Benjamin had died. Kathe was terror-stricken. God, she thought, was punishing them for her sacrifices to the pagan deity Venus (Pollock, 1989, p. 558).

Pollock explores the dark images of Kathe Kollowitz's paintings as she used them to resolve her own grief over the loss of her brother and the loss of a meaningful relationship with her mother, Katerina, who was locked in unresolved mourning. Pollock explores the complex interrelationship between mourning and creativity. "Kathe's childhood was significantly shaped by the prolonged pathological mourning of her mother, Katerina. In the case of Kathe, Katerina's failure to provide adequately warm and loving care engendered a panoply of physical and emotional symptoms including stomach pains, anxiety at losing the mother, and temper tantrums" (Pollock, 1989, p. 569). With the benefit of psychoanalytic hindsight, says Pollock, we can see beneath these symptoms not only Kathe's resentment at her mother's inability to provide empathic maternal care, but an intractable survivor guilt that paralleled the mother's equally intractable grief over the loss of Kathe's older brother.

> The images that Kathe Kollowitz uses speak to a tortured heart that lay beneath the outward flesh. Her subjects are often visibly grief-stricken, sometimes pulling or holding their faces in an attempt perhaps to contain their deep pain. The distortions, the special emphases, the expressions give us glimpses of the self of the artist that photographs and portraits by the artist other than the self artist cannot bring out. Kollowitz's art embodies a meaning that ranges beyond the personal losses of the artist. To the extent that her artistic creations are successful they constitute not only a poignant statement of her personal grief and suffering, but a successful attempt to canonize her mourning into the advocacy of certain humanitarian ideals (Pollock, 1989, p. 570).

Kathe was able to use her art to give voice to grief that had no words. She expresses on the faces of the people that she paints an unspeakable kind of pain that art has the ability to touch. Her paintings in turn draw in the viewers, who can identify with them and are touched in the same place that may lie within them.

"When a child feels they cannot reach a parent who is lost in their own grief and depression, they may feel abandoned and be plagued by fears that the parent will leave or commit suicide even if these instances do not take place. The reaction of children whose parents have divorced provoke fantasies of parental abandonment, which indeed does occur although reality says otherwise. . . ." (Pollock, 1989, p. 576). When other family members (for example, parent, siblings, grandparents) are able to maintain some semblance of continuity and cooperation, it may help alleviate some of the traumatic consequences of separation.

In the case of Rudyard Kipling, we can see how his early experience of abandonment contributed to his rich fantasy life and his ability to write wonderful, fantastical stories. Kipling's parents lived in India. At one point early in their childhood, Kipling and his sister Trix were sent to live in England at Lorn Lodge, in the care of a woman they did not know. The Kiplings felt that it was perhaps better for the children to be in England during some years of their childhood, and it is unclear why they were unaware of the abusive circumstances at Lorn Lodge, where the caretaker, Mrs. Holloway used severe and cruel forms of punishment, such as locking Rudyard in a dark and damp cellar for long periods of time to keep the young boy in line. "Kipling's fantasies in play were his salvation activity from the constant cross-examinations, punishments and humiliations. Later when his aunt asked him why he never told anyone how he was treated, he wrote 'children tell little more than animals, for what comes to them they accept as eternally established. Also, badly treated children have a clear notion of what they are likely to get if they betray the secrets of a prison house before they are clear of it'" (Pollock, 1989, p. 589). Later in Kipling's writings, readers can see both his attempt to describe his childhood humiliations and his idealization of his boyhood in India before he was sent to Lorn Lodge.

Kipling "was a man who, throughout his life, worshiped and respected (a rare combination) children and their imaginings. He took part in the children's games . . . not as so many adults, in order to impose his own scheme, but to follow and learn as well as to contribute. He would very happily leave adult company to play with children even in his 60s . . . his intense absorption could transform a small space into the whole world—much like a child does" (Pollock, 1989, p. 591).

In this image we see the imagination and the birth of play and artistry that kept the spirit of Kipling alive and free even while he was so desperately lonely and mistreated at Lorn Lodge. He was able to draw on his experiences as a young boy to develop a rich and full fantasy life that gave him respite from his hostile surroundings and later became the cornerstone upon which his art was formed (Pollock, 1989, p. 590).

In both of these lives, art was used as a special language that transformed personal pain into a universal work of art. Through their art, Kollowitz and Kipling found beauty and purpose out of struggle, a sort of artistic optimism that transcended the trials of life and turned them into a gift to the world.

Creativity and Despair

Despair has been, throughout time, a road to creativity and a path toward enlightenment or Christ consciousness. Matthew Fox says that "Christ is not only the light in all things but also the *wounds* in all things . . . the negativity path, *via negativa*, of the spiritual life [is] a path of emptying and entering the dark, trusting the dark. But also the path of suffering and letting go and bottoming out. . . . Despair is a spiritual path and [many people] do not come to spiritual experience until they enter the path of despair and disillusionment" (Fox, Sheldrake, 1996, p. 47). Despair can be a path toward deepening the container of self. Because the individual self and the cosmic self are ultimately one, contained within the very fabric of one another, composed of the same elements, using despair to deepen the self is using it to come closer to God and people.

Some of us get stuck in the idea of living in the light, as if the darkness were bad or something to be ashamed of. "Some New Agers do try to live in the light all the time. They're not living in the shadow, their own or someone else's. One way into the collective is through suffering, through that shadow" (Fox, Sheldrake, 1996, p. 127). Trying to live in the light all the time throws the personality and the mind off balance. Buddhist thought says that life should be a balance of suffering and pleasure. I think if any of us reflect for a moment, we know this in our hearts to be true, that pleasure all the time is not comfortable unless it is balanced with some other activity that is goal-oriented, that requires diligence and discipline. Merely to seek pleasure is not satisfying, and seeking to live only in the light is not natural. Balance is the key—the right balance between pleasure and struggle or between darkness and light.

There are countless examples these days of people who are channeling their grief energy toward helping others. Parents of children who have been hurt often try to aid other children, for instance. Megan Khanka's parents helped initiate Megan's Law, to enact legislation that warns of the presence of sexual offenders in order to protect other children and parents from their daughter's fate. Polly Klass's father fights for the rights of child victims of rape and abuse. Nicole Simpson's sister speaks out for battered wives. These are examples of people who are channeling their rage and despair in ways that will help others; they are memorializing the people they have lost in positive ways. They are taking the energy of their rage and pain, reinvesting in the world and making a positive contribution to themselves and others. They are working with darkness and light rather than running from it.

A Leap of Faith:
Reinvestment in the Ideal

Still another manifestation of human optimism and faith is what George Pollock refers to as a "reinvestment in the ideal." Here I cite my own grandmother. These examples of courage and faith from my own family have been a constant source of inspiration and strength in my own life. The beauty of using someone whose life has been completed is that you have access to the entire life process. My grandmother came to this country at the age of four. Her father, a wine grower and merchant in Sparta, Greece, had preceded his family to America. His vineyards had gone bad for seven years in a row, and having lost everything, he came to America to find another way to support his family. A well-to-do gentlemen from the old country, he was now ruined and faced with the need to do anything to make a living. He applied for a position as a dishwasher with a man who had picked grapes for him on his vineyards. The man was shocked and dismayed by this circumstance and said, "I cannot hire you, you were my boss, the owner of everything," to which my great-grandfather replied, "Don't think of me as who I was then but who I am now—please, I need a job." He was able to change, to reinvent himself, to use his years of business experience and eventually built three successful markets in Brooklyn, New York. My grandmother arrived in America at four years old with her two sisters and her mother, to join her father and older brothers. She relates having a pleasant childhood with loving parents. Her only sorrow, as she recalls, was growing up without a grandmother. When she complained of this to her mother, her mother would reply in Greek, "I know, darling, you weren't lucky in this."

My grandparents are the only people I know who upsized after their children left home. I believe this was both a way of enjoying their success in America, coupled with the Greek point of view that their family was not shrinking but expanding. I feel there was one other factor at play, and that is an unconscious wish on my grandmother's part to resolve her lifelong yearning *for* a grandmother by *being* a grandmother. She filled the emptiness inside of her by giving what she wished she had received, reinvesting in the ideal. My grandmother resolved her longing for a grandmother by being the grandmother she wished she had known, memorializing her lost grandmother in the daily context of life.

I believe that my grandmother learned how to reinvest in the ideal from her own parents. From her father, she witnessed a successful self-reinvention: a man who had everything, lost it all and got it back, and maintained his integrity and sense of self throughout. From her mother, I feel she was given the gift of a kind of spiritual acceptance of her fate that allowed her to reach toward resolution, unblocked by the self-pity, anger or hate that might have come had her mother steered her differently. She was allowed simply to have her pain by a sympathetic mother who did not attempt to minimize the gravity of my grand-mother's (and probably her mother's) longing. After all, her mother didn't say, "Be quiet and count your blessings." Nor did she say, "You got a raw deal, your father is to blame, rail at the fates for losing our status and wealth." She simply said, "You aren't lucky in this way." I believe framing it like that left my grandmother feeling that she was still lucky in other ways, that luck still was and could be on her side. After all, she had doting, kind-hearted parents who met all her basic needs. In other words, it did not undermine my grandmother's basic concept of herself as a lucky, blessed person.

My siblings, cousins and I were the very lucky beneficiaries of this way of resolving loss. We all adored Grammie. She was there for us unquestioningly through her life and her death. In fact, when wheeled out of the surgery that proved to announce her impending death, she looked up, disoriented, at my sister, who told her that she was in the hospital and she would stay with her. My grandmother, alerted by the word hospital, looked up at my sister and said, "Are you all right, honey?" My sister answered, "Yes, Grammie, I'm fine," at which point Grammie raised the hand without the I.V. in it, crossed herself and said, "Thank God." Her mourning had been long ago resolved. She had given what she needed to give and received what she needed to receive. She was ready to let go when we were.

Forgiving and Letting Go

One of the potential pitfalls I find when working with clients on past issues is when to put those issues to rest. This is a sticky point in anyone's process. First, because it cannot be exclusively willed— that is to say, few people can let go of the past by simply making themselves do it. Pain needs to be processed, understood and integrated back into the overall context of life in order to move on.

Forgiveness is an outgrowth of this process. When I see clients stuck and holding onto pain, we need to examine their reasons for doing so. These reasons vary. Sometimes more work is necessary to release pain, sometimes we need to explore the secondary gain that a client gets by holding onto emotional pain. People who have been traumatized develop an attachment to intense emotional states. They have, in a sense, a traumatic bond with agitated feeling states. Living without that emotional intensity can feel scary, as if their lives will feel empty and meaningless if they are not engaged in internal conflicts.

Despite this, at some point in therapy I find it is helpful to clients to subtly retrain their attitudes, trading negative thinking for optimistic thinking. There can be significant resistance around this shift. In people with childhood losses, this may be because childhood defenses were survival defenses. Letting them go can make survivors feel vulnerable and helpless. Because they were put in place early in life, personality development has been wrapped around them. The way survivors function in the world and the way they see themselves has been shaped around these defenses. It is not that they need to be eradicated. Ideally, they are resolved and reintegrated in a healthier state. But choice and attitude also play a role. There are two main pitfalls as I see it: getting stuck in the past, blaming it for all present-day ills, or denying the impact of the past and forcing a false forgiveness. Neither work. Both are a denial of self. New constructive experiences need to be introduced and undertaken so that rebuilding goes on alongside dismantling. The constructive experiences can be simulated clinically or may be part of day-to-day life. Adding an exercise program, seeking out people and situations that feel nourishing, taking up new interests and hobbies can all be a part of rebuilding a positive bank of new experience. These will act as an antidote to painful experience and can turn a life toward a positive direction.

Focusing: The Function of Goal-Setting

Though life is a journey without an end, setting goals is a way to mobilize inner power. Goals motivate us, and as long as we understand the psychological function of goal-setting, we can protect ourselves from being a slave to our own goals. The idea is to *have* a goal but not *become* the goal—not postpone living until the goal is reached.

Goals need to be "self-set" as well as imposed from the outside. When a person sets a goal of recovering from and integrating a life loss in order to live a more peaceful and productive life, that person sets his or her internal mechanisms toward that direction. It motivates toward healing. "Goals direct or steer, because in moving toward them the person makes some, rather than other, responses. And goals are functional at any given moment, because they are internal here-and-now representations of the future and not objective, actual, future events. For example, if a parent sets a standard for a child, or an employee's supervisor has an expectation of work accomplishment, neither of these external goal events are motivating unless the person internally self-sets such a goal" (Ferguson, Howell, 1994, p. 57-59).

Interestingly, it is not the achievement of the goal from which most people report the greatest satisfaction but the *process* of attaining it. Goals organize and marshal inner forces; they focus the mind. The direct engagement in an activity produces a state of what Mihaly Czikszentmihalyi of Harvard University calls *flow*—akin to a state of meditation attained by athletes, mathematicians or artists when they are fully engaged in what they are doing, fully focused in the moment (Czikszentmihalyi, 1990). In any healing journey, then, it is important for the person seeking healing to have that internal wish and motivation to self-set the goal. This will often accelerate a healing process that might otherwise be left solely to time and chance.

On the subject of death, rituals such as funerals, wakes and year-end ceremonies have addressed these issues, supplying vehicles through which to set the goal of healing, encouraging overt mourning and after a designated period of time, bringing closure to a grief process. On the subject of loss in life—losses other than death—there is little formalized ritual to turn to. Filling in these gaps and responding well to these needs are support groups, 12-Step programs, workshops, self-help literature and professional therapy. One thing that all of these modalities have in common is the recognition that healing or grieving is a process, that it occurs in real time, one day at a time.

Mature people generally realize that once they attain their aspirations, their life does not necessarily fundamentally change. However, they would also tell you that their goals motivated them toward achievement and that their achievement helped them stretch, exercise and challenge themselves to grow, to dig deep for strength and perseverance, to learn to tolerate frustration without giving up.

Belief in the Unseen

Faith, most religions tell us, is believing in what we cannot always see or prove. To go on faith is to expect a benevolent force to prevail in our life and to create a psychological condition that invites good, that awaits surprise. Rupert Sheldrake, an English physicist, suggests that though forces are unseen, they are still alive and dynamic and can be used to help us stay on a positive life trajectory.

Science in the 18th century, influenced by Descartes, led people to see the human mind as localized in particular areas of the brain, but if you search farther back into the ancient science of yoga, it will tell you that while all of the body *is* in the mind, all of the mind *is not* in the body. Mind, according to Sheldrake, is nonlocalized: It reaches outside and beyond the body.

Sheldrake, a scientist of Western thought and once-avowed atheist, traveled to India. At the time he went, he subscribed to the Western, materialistic point of view that in order to be happy we need a certain level of prosperity in our lives, that poverty equaled misery. He speaks of being both stunned and confused by what he witnessed in India—though these people lived in overwhelming poverty, they seemed to experience more joy and peace of mind than Westerners who had more than enough. "Go to the cities of Paris, London and New York and you will see harried faces," he wrote. He asked himself why a nonmaterialistic way of life could produce just the opposite effect from what, as a Westerner, he was taught it should have. Though these people had nothing, they seemed to him to be in a more satisfied state than many who had much.

Perhaps the answer lies in the fact that we are fundamentally spiritual beings—even science has caught up to this thinking now with quantum physics. When we accept the notion that our state of happiness is dependent upon how much we have, then we postpone being happy until we have it. We rely on what we have, turning our attention outward toward the accumulation of more stuff, which we believe will make us feel happy. We turn away from our inner life; we develop outer rather than inner resources. We convince ourselves that we will not be really happy until we have captured what we wish for. At first, the objects are clear: We want a car, then a house—but then wants become more subtle. We need a person or two. We need status and so on. If we would ask those people who have all of these things, they would likely tell us that it is not these things that brought them peace, but the state of "flow"—mind—that they enter in the process of working toward the goal and the fears that they conquered along the path. A goal allowed the energies of mind to organize and focus.

An Attitude of Gratitude

One line has always struck a chord with me in 12-Step rooms: "Ours is a disease of attitudes." Negative, pessimistic, twisted thinking gets us all into trouble. What situation in life is helped by a negative attitude? And yet we hold onto it, defend it and allow it to consume our thinking. We convince ourselves that negative thinking is just being realistic, but is this really what we want our reality to look like? Recently, I heard an interview with a man who has had two children born HIV-positive. When asked how he lives with this tragedy, he said, "Well, you can take a victim attitude and say 'why me?' or you can take it as a challenge and say 'why not me?' " Life isn't fair. If it were, why shouldn't we be starving and watching our children starve in Africa, or why aren't we in Bosnia losing our homes, our relatives and the life we hold dear? Feeling that we should get though this life without problems is unrealistic thinking. In fact, life is so full of potential pitfalls that our best chance at a happy life lies in learning early on how to manage adversity, how to find it within ourselves to accept and deal with difficult circumstances.

Praise and celebration are, and have been throughout history, ways of tuning in with and appreciating life. They are ways of growing the soul. "Eckhart says that God is delighted when your soul grows bigger and bigger, which is another way of say-ing that it's time to grow soul," says Matthew Fox.

> We have trivialized soul not only in the physiological and mechanistic sense, but in every other sense too. Our souls shriv-eled up during the Cartesian era. If you're cut off from the souls of all the other animals and plants and beings and stars, you're just hiding away in your own little man-made space. It's not even a space, it's a place. No wonder we have *acedia* (boredom), that sin that comes, as Aquinas says, from the shrinking of the soul, the shrinking of the mind. We have shrunk our souls. That's the process of the last three centuries. That's why we can tear down rain forests, destroy our nest, kill the children to come and not think of it, and can say we're all holy and happy and full of bliss. We're out of touch with our own grief! We are separated from the responsibility for our own actions and our connection to all the joy and pain in the world. All this is about souls that have shrunk up. This is why we're into addiction—we're covering up the truth of our shrunken souls with everything from liquor to drugs to television to shopping to sex to anything (Fox, Sheldrake, 1996, p. 83, 84).

It is difficult to grow soul in a world that has shrunk the dimensions of the soul and forgotten that without it, life is only an empty shell. But everywhere around us is a thirst to grow soul, to grow self. One way to grow soul is through grief and suffering. Few of us come to spirit spontaneously these days. Many of us enter the realm of growing soul and spirit through suffering. Anger, rage and self-pity are an early and natural part of the grief experience, but they need to be moved through into sorrow and then transcendence in order for the grief experience to be a path toward enlarging the soul. Rupert Sheldrake and Matthew Fox feel that there need to be rituals to deal with this anger and rage so that they come out of the body and bring the feeling to the surface. Experiential therapy and psychodrama allow for the open catharsis of these emotions. One Native American ritual is to psychologically put anger into a stone, then wrap and bury the stone and give the anger to the universe—to turn it over. Sheldrake says,

> I like the idea of these rituals. Anger and resentment, like other patterns of emotional response, are not merely personal; they have a generic, habitual quality. For example, if you get into a resentful state of mind, simply by being in that state of mind you tune in by *morphic resonance* [energy field] with countless people who have been resentful in the past, including yourself. So you are actually influenced by your own past resentments and resentments many other people have felt. You tune into a generalized sense of resentment. These things are transpersonal in the sense that they possess us. We're not usually very original. Most of the feelings, habits, states of mind we get into, many other people have had in the past. When we get into them we're linking ourselves to all the people who have been in similar states before us (Fox, Sheldrake, 1996, p. 98).

If you accept Sheldrake's theory of morphic resonance, suddenly it makes sense why good thinking and clean and wholesome living lead to more of that, and negative pessimistic living leads to more painful living. Simply by placing ourselves on a positive path, we are helped by the countless number of souls who have walked that path before us, be it a positive or negative path. Through this phenomenon of morphic resonance, through this subtle field of energy connection, we can enlist the help of other unseen energy fields—what Joseph Campbell called being "helped and carried by invisible hands." Praise and celebration, being grateful and appreciating the gift of life and the mystery of the universe, are part of what make us aware that we are actually living life and help us to become responsible and grateful for the life we have been given—what Fox describes as the sense of awe and the sense of the sacred in all that is alive. More and more, soul is being seen as the animating principle inherent in all things. So we are animated by soul: a sunrise, a church group or a 12-Step meeting, the trees, the birds and the magic of a beautiful morning are all brought to life through the energy and mystery of soul. When we stand in awe, when we feel our feelings and care for the feelings of others, when we are deeply moved by mountains, animals or human tears, we are growing soul.

As Archbishop Desmond Tutu says, "Blocks and adversity are not meant to stop you, they are meant to challenge you to overcome them." We grow *through* not *in spite of.* We use the stuff of this world and the experiences of it to challenge and expand our own perceptions, to enlarge our hearts, and in so doing we *become*—we become more spiritual, we develop ego strength, we become deeper, wiser and more in tune. Whatever situation we are given, we have a choice: to move through it or to shut down. Anger and resentment are natural. They are part of a process of grieving and letting go, but they are only part of the process. We are meant to fully feel our anger and rage, to own it, embrace it, and feel the sorrow and confusion beneath it, to fully enter into our own pain so that we can transcend it through experiencing it. Trying to transcend it without feeling it just doesn't work; it then gets lived out in the arena of our relationships in painful, alienating ways. We need to be willing to look bad, to feel bad, to say the wrong thing, to be awkward, to fail, but to try—to do our share in bumbling through to the other side of a conflict.

People with addictions have one of the most beautiful, spiritual networks in the world to help them weather this process, to provide them with support, wisdom and eventually a design for living that can enrich their lives from then on. Because that's what's underneath healing from addiction anyway—a need for a design for living, for learning how to live in tune with soul and spirit rather than out of tune. I myself have gone to Al-Anon for many years in order to come to accept my father's drinking and to understand what it did to our family. Countless times I hear people express gratitude to the disease that has taught them so much, that brought them into a spiritually oriented fellowship that opened their hearts to love, understanding and forgiveness. Working through the pain of an addicted loved one brought us all closer to our own personal truth, toward the beauty in living even though life was and is not perfect and predictable. Grief is actually a path to letting go. Letting go is part of the spiritual path—letting go of personal limitations and pessimistic thinking about life and relationships. Shifting thinking into a positive frame of mind, if you subscribe to the theory of morphic resonance, can enlist help from unseen sources.

The theory of "brain set" put forward by Peter Russell sheds light on a positive attitude that can help us to use the world constructively. Brain set, like mental set, is our accepted way of seeing ourselves. For example, people who see themselves as lucky will tend to interpret circumstances as lucky that another might not, while people with a defeatist brain set tend to interpret events to reinforce this defeatist brain set. Each person will scan the environment for situations that match up to his or her particular set and will use those circumstances to add to that individual self-concept as a "lucky" or an "unlucky" person. Naturally identifying positive experiences is the first step toward bringing them into our lives (Russell, 1979, p. 211-223).

In My End Is My Beginning:
Why Is an Inner Death a Gateway to Life?

It is only through experiencing small and large inner deaths that anyone can say yes to life and relationships in all their complexity. With all its disillusionments, it is still life—a mysterious and beautiful journey . . . our journey. The willingness to work through a process of grieving and mourning life's losses is what allows us to reinvent ourselves at each new stage of living. At the heart of spiritual transformation, *the self is engaged in the cycle of living death, rebirth,* and *transformation* over and over again. It is what gives life purpose and meaning and what keeps us young.

Current research shows us that old information presented in a new way, or games that stimulate new thinking, cause new brain cell growth and ward off diseases of aging such as Alzheimer's. Openness to the self in all its wondrous variety is mental and emotional exercise at the deepest level. The ability to *unearth*, *excavate* and *examine* buried material from the deep waters of the unconscious is what researchers are finding strengthens our immune systems and even wards off disease. To know the self, to embark on a sincere path of self-study, enables us to walk the path of life as living souls. When we are current with ourselves psychologically and emotionally, we live in the here and now, the sacred and alive moment—we are in tune. From a current inner space we can walk through the world as a traveler, knowing we are here for a limited time, and we can appreciate life as the journey without a goal that it really is. It is, after all, the process of living itself, as Joseph Campbell puts it, "the being in touch with the eternal aspect in the temporal moment," that gives life its spirituality. To hide from parts of our inner world, to disown and disacknowledge what we carry in the depths of our own heart, is to close the door on living. The danger we fear is that in opening Pandora's box, we will become lost in pain and rage—that we will submit to our baser nature—but it is the very refusal of our dark side that gives it power. We are, alas, human and perhaps only truly appreciate what is hard-won—even when what we are winning is another piece of self, of inner freedom, of jurisdiction over and acceptance of our own inner world.

In Al-Anon we learn to surrender control and to turn over to God a problem that we may not be able to carry alone. We develop a sort of partnership with God in working through our daily affairs, inviting God's presence and light into a space within us that was once isolated and dark. We experience, first-hand, the transformative power of a grief experience by inviting God and other people to play a role in its resolution, recognizing that resolution lies as much in seeing it differently as in changing or controlling outside people and events. We learn that another person's disease does not have to become ours. As powerful as addiction is, God and community are stronger.

Today While the Blossoms Still Cling to the Vine: Grief and Living in the Present

We bond to our families, we take important people into ourselves by modeling, and we integrate careers, lifestyles and routines that when changed, lost or disrupted, cause pain. The mother who treats her adult children in the same manner that she treated them when they were young and who cannot transition into seeing them as adult people, the CEO who is unable to feel good about himself outside of his work role, or the perennial campus hero who throughout life continues to pigeonhole people by where they went to college are examples of people whose identities have become fixed. The intimate relationship that functions but does not live, that maintains itself but does not allow those in it to change and grow, is a testimony to a fixed status quo. Changing from one role and moving into another can feel threatening. However, we suffer a loss of personal spontaneity when we are stuck at various points along the timeliness of our own lives. Spontaneity allows us to have an adequate and appropriate response to a given situation, neither too much nor too little.

Meditation in Action

One of the gifts of releasing preoccupations that bind energy is that energy can be freed up and used to infuse the daily rituals of life with a higher sense of meaning. It is not life that changes, necessarily, but our way of relating to the life that we already have. I find it useful to set aside some time during the day simply to enter into a sort of state of reverie, to tap into the spirituality that exists in the moment. If I neglect the importance of this simple practice, days can go by when I forget to appreciate the beauty in everyday living. Spirituality is always present, waiting for me to connect with it, but I need to consciously make that connection. I find breathing and quiet very useful. Quieting my breath allows spirit to enter my being in a natural sort of way. Then I direct my mind toward seeing the circumstances of my life in a positive light, and I allow spirit to wrap itself around the moment, to weave its way into my contemplation. I picture situations not only as they are, but as I would like them to be. I allow myself to see the dream fulfilled and then I place it in the hands of God, trusting that God's sense of timing and what is right for me is better than my own.

I turn over my desire to the loving hands of my Higher Power and I psychologically place those I love in those same hands. If I have a circumstance that needs solving, I take the actions necessary to resolve it that are within my power. Then, I do my best to let go of the results. Perhaps there are aspects of a situation that I cannot fully see or understand at this time, but I feel that if I put it in God's hands after I have done all that I can, that we are working as a team—I will do what I can and let God do the rest. But I must do the asking. I know in my heart that God wishes to help me and all people, but I know that it is my job to ask for that help. I'll never forget a Hindu priest I met in India who said that, "For every one step we take toward God, God will take four toward us." I have found this to be true in my life and when I feel that God is not working in my life, I quiet down, do my meditation and remember that I have forgotten to ask, to place my hand in God's so that we can walk together.

Rabbi Daniel I. Schwartz refers to the practice of joy as a deep-down satisfaction that comes from "collaborating with God in our Destiny." Any activity undertaken with love can become a meditation in action. In her book, *The Knitting Sutra,* Susan Gordon Aleyden describes how a hobby can bring meaning.

> Consider a grandmother knitting a sweater for a grandchild just coming into the world. In the stitches of that sweater go all the grandmother's prayers for a safe delivery, all of her good feelings about the child and its parents. The work itself is a prayer for the safety and well-being of the mother and child, a labor of love, a ritual welcoming of new life inside the extended family or tribe. . . . The purpose of the work is not so much to make beautiful things as to become beautiful inside while you are making those things . . . consider what meanings you attach to your favorite hobby . . . identify how it reflects your understanding of the sacred (Aleyden, 1997).

Standing in the Wound: How Do We Process Painful Feelings?

Alvin Toffler, in *Future Shock,* said that in the house of the future every home should have a psychodrama stage on which each family member could safely give voice to the deepest parts of the self. Dr. J. L. Moreno, the father of psychodrama, said, "The stage is enough"—each one of us needs a stage on which to explore ourselves, on which to unbridle our irrational inner voices, to be, in turn, clumsy or magnificent. There we can walk out of our numbness, out of psychic sleep, out of soul death and into life, into being. When we can find the safe and structured expression for the hurt inner child, the ambitious, driven power-monger, the bitch, the angel, the starving or gorging self, we can unmuzzle these subselves and give them a moment to be and breathe: We can do our acting out on the stage of healing, rather than on the stage of life. We can bring our complexes, drives and passions into action where they will not hurt, wound and destroy ourselves and those we love.

Sometimes trauma survivors dissociate from memory. It is stored in the brain out of conscious awareness—that is, the observing self or the part of us that watches from within is disengaged. The memory therefore does not get integrated into a working model of the self; you might say it is out of sight but not fully out of mind. Generally people carrying dissociated memories have a vague sense that some hidden truth lurks within them that, if revealed, would be frightening. It almost feels as if something happened to a different self. Integrating these memories requires feeling the pain, fear and vulnerability that were put out of consciousness at the moment of trauma, or during the issue or relationship dynamic over which they experienced trauma. When one member of a couple gets consistently triggered by the other and flies into a rage or a sea of tears or shuts down, it may be the psyche's way of trying to access the hidden truth, to reveal it, to let it out. When we are no longer living in fear of our own disowned insides, we are free to look at life with a detached sort of wisdom, an acceptance of who we are. We have seen the worst and it didn't kill us—we are ready to live.

Consider the case of Sophie: Sophie describes a suitcase that she kept packed and ready to go as a nine-year-old. Sometimes she was dropped off with aunts and uncles for weeks or months. Sometimes with neighbors. Once she came home from school and found that her parents had moved and neglected to tell her. She went to a pay phone and called a friend who eventually tracked down her parents, but no explanations were offered that could have helped Sophie put this event into a recognizable context. Rather, she was left to construct her own meaning with a child's mind. Not surprisingly, she simply went numb. The harsh reality that her two alcoholic parents who were once again fleeing a hounding landlord and were too overwhelmed with their own life problems to remember her was understandably beyond the reach of her childlike capacity for reasoning. Instead, she came to the conclusion that a small child in these circumstances all too often arrives at: "I was not worth remembering, I am not important to my parents." When she stayed with her older sister, who tried to step in for her parents, she kept her suitcase hidden under her bed so the landlady wouldn't think she was living there. She kept herself hidden too. She was in therapy for at least 18 months before the numbness wore off enough for her to recall, in fits and starts, these heart-wrenching testimonies of her lost childhood. Sophie learned to hide her terror, her confusion, her pleasures and her dreams. She learned to quietly attach herself to anyone who seemed interested enough to take care of her.

Sophie was an opera singer. She took up this profession because someone who cared about her encouraged her to do it. Singing was a boat to somewhere, a reaching out for direction and community, an attempt to fill the terrifying void her two alcoholic parents had left her in as a child. Sophie left home at 17 and went to work as a nanny, looking after the two children of an opera singer—it was a new hope, a new possibility of being safe, of getting taken care of. It worked for a while. Six or seven years later, Sophie entered therapy because she finally had the time. She had injured her voice and could no longer sing. The profession she had chosen was a good solution but not a complete one; she needed to go back to the child who lived silently within her—to let that child sing too, to let her come out of hiding and find a voice that was hers and could be valued and sustained. Sophie's task was to grieve not only what she lost but all that she never had. We walked Sophie through the stages of grieving. First the numbness wore off and she was flooded with deep feelings. The yearning she felt for what she had lost was almost unbearable at times. Her life felt derailed—like a train going nowhere—until finally the fog lifted and she started to take up residence in her own life, to live in her own body. As her self began filling in, her voice also started healing. Her path was one of deep mourning, not for an outer death but an inner one.

In her intimate relationships, Sophie anxiously attached herself to people she perceived as powerful and capable of taking care of her—most memorably a married, unavailable man whom she fantasized would one day leave his wife and choose her. This never happened and she was left, once again, lonely and alone. However, Sophie's case is a happy one. Her mourning process returned her not only to the person she feared she had lost but to a beautiful, gifted young woman who reclaimed a successful career and relationship with a life partner. The mourning process is rational, and once begun develops a life of its own that is self-curative if not complicated by other factors. In Sophie's case, she sought the professional help she needed to work through the complications so that mourning could be fully beneficial. Sophie became her own best advocate in rebuilding her life. She expresses this process with clarity and wisdom in the following words.

When I began to study developmental theory and ego psychology, I read Eda Goldstein on the interrelated process of social work practice; "restore, maintain, enhance." I was stunned to find words that so concisely described what I had been through. Having dismantled and then reassembled the fragmented pieces of myself, I began to feel restored to a sense of wholeness and found a renewed ability to know "basic trust."

Because I grew up around substance abuse, I had adopted many distorted concepts, destructive attitudes and negative thinking. I lived, as George Eliot wrote, "in that roar which lies on the other side of silence." It took great effort to put myself forward in a proactive, self-affirming way. I had a steady support system that affirmed, nurtured and—most important—stood witness, as I uncovered, acknowledged and expressed the truth of my personal history. This helped me build a bridge back to life—from coping to adapting. I was taught how to identify and articulate feelings and needs; I was encouraged to express those needs; I was challenged to make choices and take risks that lead to building competence. I began to feel a sense of purpose. In further study of Erikson, Mahler and Winnicott, I recognized that the tenets of the recovery process parallel the developmental model in which, ideally, people incorporate ego strength as they build upon each previous stage of their life.

I first began taking classes in order to explore what other talents and skills I could develop. I took a course at the New School to train as a teacher for English as a Second Language. I have become an ongoing volunteer at Symphony Space Theater at their performances for children as well as their "Selected Shorts" evenings. These experiences are extremely rewarding because they allow me to be part of and give service in a multi-ethnic community that offers a vast variety of programming to many different cultures.

I also worked at the Dialogue House, which sponsored the Intensive Journal Program. This writing program was created by Ira Progoff and is based on his work with Carl Jung. The Journal Program has been extremely useful for many people, myself included, as a therapeutic tool because it offers a structured method of working with one's inner voices in a nonjudgmental written dialogue.

Sophie learned to find experiences in the outside world that fed her inner world, satisfying her hunger for place, meaning and connection with what appealed to her own sense of taste.

Inner Dramas: Hungers for Action

We carry within the self inner dramas, unsatisfied hungers for action that come forward in the form of reenactments in life. Impulses from the unconscious relate to parts of ourselves that yearn for expression and fulfillment. This expression can be positive or negative, creative or destructive. We all share pain. No one is without it, but the choice is in how we seek to resolve that pain. In that choice live the old and the new narrative. The old narrative is the old interpretation, how we interpreted the events of our lives and how we continue to live by those interpretations. The child who was told that he was of mediocre intelligence, who continues to live life as if he were in his total being confined to a mediocre life, is living by the old interpretation and making it a lifelong script. In that now-adult man's new narrative, he needs to reframe the old interpretation. Perhaps the reframe is in recognizing that school did not motivate him, that sitting in classes in which he was expected to listen and then repeat what he had heard was not engaging for him. That sitting still and listening hour after hour did not satisfy his need to integrate and express knowledge in a way that was meaningful to him. He can learn, as an adult, to seek out those learning experiences that turn him on and satisfy his way of processing information. He can learn to see that the school system was just that—the school system, not the entire world—and he can release himself from the way that it defined him, and release himself into the rest of the world and his own learning style.

This redefining occurs on an emotional level as well. Children grow up seeing themselves in the way that they are seen by those who raised them. This is how self-image is in part formed; we take on the way those closest saw us as our own self-concept, internalizing their voices and accepting their opinions of us as our opinions of ourselves. This becomes very evident in the psychodramas that I do with clients. When a client casts others to play his father, mother and siblings, he has a chance to see again what he got, since in psychodrama he is the one who scripts the scene. He gets the situation replayed or played back to him as he originally experienced it, thus giving him a second look at the interpretations he made at the time about himself. Then he can have a corrective experience, reconstructing the scene or metaphor of his life in the way that he wished it had been, thus creating a new synthetic memory to store alongside the old one, so that when the old one gets triggered the new one will hopefully help counter it. It is a marvelous method for getting a look at the self in action. Unfortunately, psychodrama got confused with the intense encounter therapy so popular in the 1970s. But psychodrama is a highly evolved role-playing method. J. L. Moreno, the father of psychodrama, is in fact the father of role-playing methods currently in use all over the world, and also of group therapy. Until this point, therapy had been seen as an exclusively one-to-one process. But Moreno observed children playing in the parks of Vienna, and he envisioned that adults, too, might benefit from taking on roles, playing first the self and then reversing roles and playing another person, looking back at the self or playing out the various aspects or roles within the self.

As we have discussed, we make meaning out of loss, whether that be a loss of family, job or a spouse. The meaning that we make is subjective—it is based on what we accepted as true at that time and the meaning, interpretation and response to the event by the other people surrounding it.

The little girl whose father left the family may come to see relationships with men as temporary. A relationship in her mind can be synonymous with pain, conflict and eventual abandonment. When she grows up, if there were no subsequent experiences to alter that perception, she may see all men as too risky to depend upon and fear marriage and commitment. If this girl is able to process the loneliness and sorrow over the loss of her father, she will have less need to project that grief onto all men. She can have the insight that all men are not her father and can begin to look for other models of ways to be a father, thus changing the meaning "all men will abandon" to "some men abandon but most do not." She may also develop a special sensitivity to people in pain and help others work through an experience that she now has worked through and moved on from. Relationships may seem all the more precious to her, as she is now in touch with the real meaning of commitment and caring from having lived without it.

Creating a new narrative allows us to make our own meaning and to see the events of life in a way that allows us to grow from them rather than to be a victim of circumstance. Many people do this naturally—the rest of us can benefit from a little help. But all of us have the capacity to turn the prism over and over again in our mind's eye until we are able to see the situation in a new light. After all, "life," as Emerson says "is an angle of vision." It is how we see our lives that allows us to see the same glass of water as half-full that another person might insist is half-empty.

There also exists a sleeping sickness of the soul. Its most dangerous aspect is that one is unaware of its coming. That is why you have to be careful. . . . You should realize that your soul suffers if you live superficially. People need times in which to concentrate, when they can search their innermost selves. It is tragic that most men have not achieved this teaching of self-awareness. And finally, when they hear the inner voice they do not want to listen anymore. They carry on as before so as not to be constantly reminded of what they lost. But as for you, resolve to keep a quiet time. . . . Then your souls can speak to you without being drowned out by the hustle and bustle of everyday life (Schweitzer, n.d.).

PART V

The Personal Journey

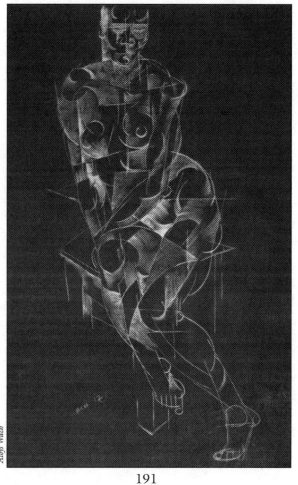

Aloys Wach

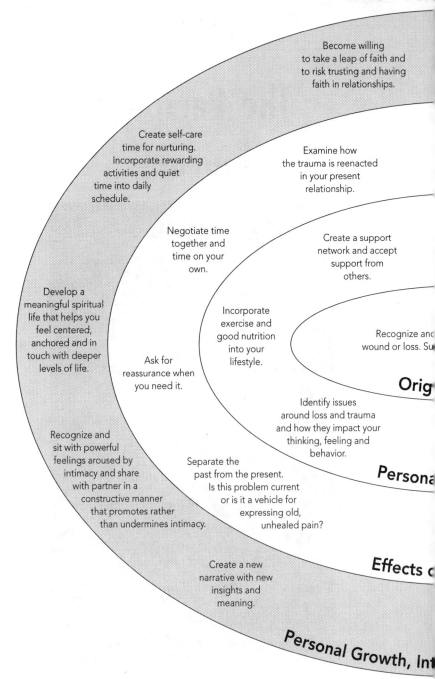

The Path

Become willing to take a leap of faith and to risk trusting and having faith in relationships.

Create self-care time for nurturing. Incorporate rewarding activities and quiet time into daily schedule.

Examine how the trauma is reenacted in your present relationship.

Negotiate time together and time on your own.

Create a support network and accept support from others.

Develop a meaningful spiritual life that helps you feel centered, anchored and in touch with deeper levels of life.

Incorporate exercise and good nutrition into your lifestyle.

Ask for reassurance when you need it.

Recognize and wound or loss. Su

Orig

Identify issues around loss and trauma and how they impact your thinking, feeling and behavior.

Recognize and sit with powerful feelings aroused by intimacy and share with partner in a constructive manner that promotes rather than undermines intimacy.

Separate the past from the present. Is this problem current or is it a vehicle for expressing old, unhealed pain?

Persona

Effects

Create a new narrative with new insights and meaning.

Personal Growth, Int

f Healing

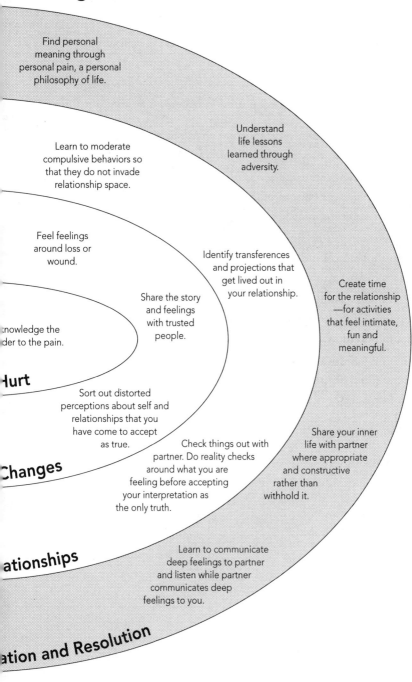

Find personal meaning through personal pain, a personal philosophy of life.

Understand life lessons learned through adversity.

Learn to moderate compulsive behaviors so that they do not invade relationship space.

Feel feelings around loss or wound.

Identify transferences and projections that get lived out in your relationship.

Create time for the relationship —for activities that feel intimate, fun and meaningful.

Share the story and feelings with trusted people.

knowledge the der to the pain.

Hurt

Sort out distorted perceptions about self and relationships that you have come to accept as true.

Check things out with partner. Do reality checks around what you are feeling before accepting your interpretation as the only truth.

Share your inner life with partner where appropriate and constructive rather than withhold it.

Changes

Learn to communicate deep feelings to partner and listen while partner communicates deep feelings to you.

ationships

ation and Resolution

wounds

With the drawing of this love
And the voice of this loving
We shall not cease from exploration
And the end of all our exploring
Will be to arrive where we started
And know the place for the first time
Through the unknown, remembered gate.

T. S. Eliot

The Personal Journey

How to Use Process Pages

O n the following pages you will find a variety of options for constructing what I term "process pages." These exercises and dialogues are meant to help you embrace your own sense of loss and grief and move through the stages that lead to healing. These exercises are voluntary, not compulsory. Do them if you feel drawn to do so, or read through them and simply enjoy them as other people's journeys that may shed light on your own. The goal of doing these exercises is simple. They are meant to help you allow your feelings and ideas to flow freely; each "process page" exercise can be uninhibited, unedited and free-flowing. What you will discover is that you and all of us are selves in process. These exercises will allow you to get to know and express the different parts of yourself. In the act of doing that, you can choose to deal with painful memories and feelings in a new way. Choice is often the result of seeing the different parts of yourself more clearly.

Each of us has a part of our minds that observes. Each of us has an inner witness. Journaling strengthens the inner witness by allowing us to observe our own thoughts and feelings. It helps us integrate thoughts we have relegated to semiconsciousness or repressed along with more conscious thoughts. We hear through the process of defensive exclusion. This theory holds that part of the mind stands at the gateway of consciousness making split-second decisions as to what material will be taken in consciously and what material will be relegated to psychic storage bins or filing cabinets. Journaling trains the mind to observe its own process, which aids in the integration of both conscious and semiconscious thoughts. People who understand their own insides are in a better position to make the kinds of choices both on a daily basis and for a larger life plan that are tailored to suit their particular needs and wishes.

We are attempting to embrace rather than run from pain, to use pain as fertilizer for growing soul. In this act we are saying yes not only to the joy of life but also to the wounds of life. It is through our woundedness that we connect with our deeper selves and with spirit. This journal journey is a path home toward self. The natural benefit is that by penetrating the mystery of self, we penetrate the mystery of life and God because when all is said and done, it is all connected. We are meant to be here, we are meant to use self as our own personal vehicle to the Divine Spirit, and the Divine Spirit is meant to use each and every person as the vehicle through which spirit is made manifest.

So when you write, keep it simple. Put your pen to paper and let go. Don't think; just write. These pages are for your eyes only, unless you choose to share them. Let the paper be your friend and pour your heart out onto the page. Through free-writing, you will find that your thoughts unravel by themselves. All you have to do is allow them to come forward onto the paper. Just relax and enjoy the process.

The following guidelines will illuminate the approximate stages of recovery over loss and trauma. The stages are fluid, not fixed, and can be repeated, collided or leapfrogged. By understanding these overall stages you will also have a framework for understanding the goal of doing your "process pages." It is natural to go through these stages in one form or other as we face our own pain, and it can be comforting to know when you feel stuck that you are only in a stage of the process and that you can progress. So *first,* you acknowledge the loss. This allows you to identify the loss issue that is at the core of the painful feelings. *Second,* you tell your story, and by doing so you bear witness to your own pain and begin to accept support. As you feel and share the feelings surrounding both the current loss and the early loss, you begin to make this process real to yourself, by witnessing your own experience, and you allow others to act as a witness to validate your experience of pain. *Third,* you start linking current behavior with the original trauma or cumulative traumas. Now you can begin making the connection between the current life behavior or emotional symptoms and the original trauma or cumulative traumas. *Fourth,* a turning point comes when you can separate the past experience from the present emotional agitation. By separating the emotional and psychological overreactions in the present from their root cause in the past, you begin integrating the sense of loss into your present inner psychological and emotional world. *Finally,* you create a new narrative; this new inner life story includes new insight, new awareness, new meaning. You can see the old pain through the new present-day lens, placing it in the overall context of your life, which allows you to reinvest energy into living today.

Process Pages As Dialogues and Exercises

The following 16 exercises and dialogues are in no magical order. In fact, it may be helpful to browse through the different options and start with one that draws you and seems most interesting or doable to you. Everyone is in a different place on this journey, and only you know what best addresses your own pain. Embracing pain is work. Few of us want to do this; we all would rather live in a certain amount of denial. But eventually that denial becomes counterproductive. The pain that we won't face comes up out of the past and the unconscious and sabotages present-day living experiences and relationships. Even if you think you should have already "worked through" any pain over some loss in the past, the residue of trauma can be present on a subtle level. So do these exercises at your own pace. It may also be helpful to have a friend or group to share in the work of doing this. If you don't want to share what you have actually written, you may still want to discuss how you felt about doing the exercise or share some lesson you learned from embracing and writing about your pain and grief.

At the core of this kind of work is the process of dialogue. In other words, you engage in a conversation with different parts of yourself, or with people from your past *as you remember them,* which is the key distinction. It is how you remember them and how you remember the way you interacted with them that still may be affecting you. It is the truth that you carry within yourself, and as such it needs to be honored and processed. The process of dialogue is illuminating and difficult. It brings insight, and eventually it gives you choices. You can choose how to work with your pain, how to heal, what help you need and at what pace you want to move along this healing journey.

So on the following pages you will find: 1) a loss chart that you can fill out; 2) a grief questionnaire that you can complete; 3) a dialogue writing exercise around a photograph; 4) a dialogue writing exercise with the most silent part of yourself; 5) a dialogue writing exercise with your body; 6) a dialogue writing exercise with a wounded part of yourself; 7) a dialogue writing exercise with your "shadow" side, or the "unwanted" part of yourself; 8) a dream dialogue; 9) a letter-writing exercise with a significant person in your past; 10) a learning-by-imitation monologue exercise; 11) a writing exercise to understand the dynamic of "projection"; 12) a writing exercise for clarifying beliefs and perceptions; 13) an episode from your own story writing exercise; 14) a time-line chart to fill in your personal history of loss or trauma; 15) an empowerment writing exercise; 16) a letter to God writing exercise.

Remember, these are exercises for promoting growth and healing; they are not tests. No one is looking over your shoulder, no one is grading you. This is just an opportunity to courageously face your own life and begin to take the steps necessary to heal yourself if you wish to. This is an act of self-affirmation that will take you deeper into yourself and deeper into the mystery of divine spirit. You may also wish to simply read through the examples given and see which ones you identify with. Use this last section in any way that best suits *you!*

EXERCISE 1

The Loss Chart

Goal: To focus on the current loss that is creating inner anxiety, agitation or turmoil and to reveal the links it has to the losses in all of your life and history.

Requirements: The Loss Chart form and the Loss Chart form example.

Instructions: In the empty circle on page 202 write in the loss that you are currently focusing on for this exercise. On the lines emanating from the circle allow yourself to "free associate," to fill in the actual life incidents and/or feelings that arise around this loss. Some thoughts will be related to this loss and some may be related to previous losses. In other words, don't criticize yourself or block any feelings or ideas that spontaneously emerge. Just follow one feeling or thought to the next. Stop at any point, or when you think or feel that you would like to take the exercise to a deeper place by using one of the other exercises to complete the process.

Sample: See the completed chart that precedes the blank chart.

◆

Loss Chart Example

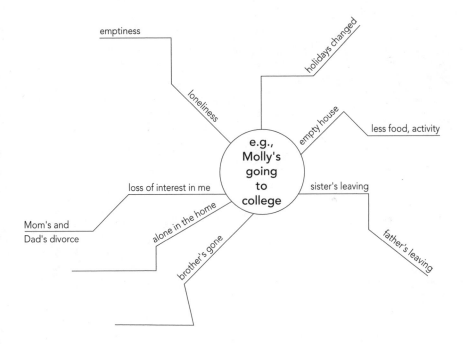

Loss Chart

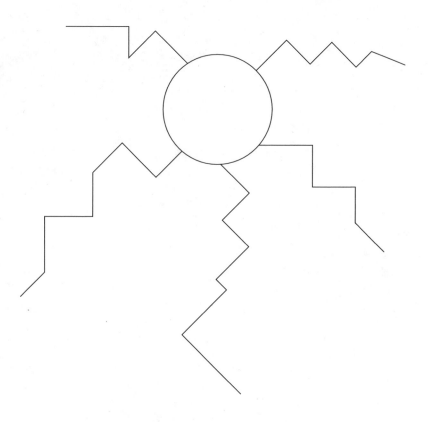

EXERCISE 2

The Grief Questionnaire

Goal: This questionnaire is designed to give you more information about your current loss and to heighten your awareness of the role that unresolved grief may be playing in your life.

Requirements: The Grief Questionnaire form.

Instructions: First determine the issue that you have decided is your current concern. Then answer these questions by placing a check in the box that represents your experience most closely.

Sample: See the completed questionnaire that follows the blank form.

◆

Grief Test

	Very Little	Somewhat	Quite A Bit	Very Much
1. How much do you feel unresolved emotions surrounding this loss?	❑	❑	❑	❑
2. How disrupted in your daily routines do you feel?	❑	❑	❑	❑
3. How much depression do you feel?	❑	❑	❑	❑
4. How much yearning do you feel?	❑	❑	❑	❑
5. How much emotional constriction do you experience?	❑	❑	❑	❑

	Very Little	Somewhat	Quite a Bit	Very Much
6. How much sadness do you feel?	❏	❏	❏	❏
7. How much anger do you feel?	❏	❏	❏	❏
8. How much ghosting (continued psychic presence) of the lost person, situation or part of self do you feel?	❏	❏	❏	❏
9. How much fear of the future do you feel?	❏	❏	❏	❏
10. How much trouble are you having organizing yourself?	❏	❏	❏	❏
11. How uninterested in your life do you feel?	❏	❏	❏	❏
12. How much old, unresolved grief is being activated and remembered as a result of this current issue?	❏	❏	❏	❏
13. How tired do you feel?	❏	❏	❏	❏
14. How much hope do you feel about your life and the future?	❏	❏	❏	❏
15. How much regret do you feel?	❏	❏	❏	❏
16. How much self-recrimination do you feel?	❏	❏	❏	❏
17. How much shame or embarrassment do you feel?	❏	❏	❏	❏

This test is designed to heighten awareness of the role that unresolved grief over a loss is playing in your life. You may wish to use your process pages to journal about feelings that arise or share the feelings in a support group.

◆

EXERCISE 3

The Photograph Dialogue

Goal: By selecting a photograph of yourself at some point in your life that speaks to you, you can illuminate issues and feelings related to that time in your life. By creating a dialogue with yourself as depicted in the picture at the time the photograph was taken and then as you are today, you can begin to understand how a circumstance may have affected you.

Requirements: Choose a photograph that draws you for whatever reason, whether it is happy or sad. You also need a journal for chronicling the dialogue, either on paper or electronically.

Instructions: Place the photograph in a position where it can be viewed throughout this process.

1. Now write a monologue, speaking as yourself, as you are represented in the photograph. Tell others about yourself, introducing yourself as you are in the photo, describing your thoughts and feelings, again as you appear in the photo.

2. Now write a dialogue; converse with yourself, as the person in the photo and the person you are today. Be sure to express both sets of feelings and thoughts. You have just spoken "as" yourself. Now write a dialogue speaking "to" yourself.

3. Place your photo in the designated place and answer the questions that appear on page 209. You may wish to share your answers with an appropriate person or group.

Sample:

1. (An excerpt)

My name is Lynette, and this is a picture of me with my mother and my in-laws. I am an actor and singer but I am on "vocal silence" during this time. The doctor has ordered me to be quiet for a whole week. This to me does not feel like a punishment, but rather a freedom. I am not required to make any small talk. I am not allowed to find anything witty to say, nor to argue any points with anyone. My only job is to listen and observe, take it all in without anyone knowing what I am thinking or who I am thinking about. They do not even know if I am with them. I could be in Barbados lying naked on a beach, but smiling and nodding in front of them. How strange, then, that I should look so happy, for I thought I would be a bit nervous to be with my mother during a time of silence because she does not understand rules and usually ignores them.

Yet my smile is genuine when I see her. And I want to show her off to my new family. And I feel safe and secure, protected here in their house, not hers, so she has to be easy-going and let others take the lead more. And she has even let down her hair a bit, she looks somewhat messy, and admits that she is tired and that she cannot go out dancing because she needs to sleep. And she wakes up late and comes out in her bathing suit though her stomach is flabby, and we swim together. And when Jean brings out hummus and pizza, she digs right in. And she does not demand too often that I speak to her, nor does she do anything but giggle when I strongly shake that I cannot. And she plays with Danny, my nephew, in a very neutral way tonight, not like she knows best how to be with kids, and he likes the French chocolate she has brought, a gift appropriate for a spontaneous occasion, not too big. And she seems relaxed, and I am affectionate with her. It feels nice to be with Mommy. To have a mommy. And even to have this woman be that mommy. I don't feel young or old, just like a daughter with her mom, maybe even looking up to her mom. I do not really feel like telling her any of this because I am so enjoying just feeling it all, and also because I can't use my voice anyway. I do tell her repeatedly how happy I am that she came, because at first she felt she would be an imposition, but I wish I could find words to better express the depth of my happiness with our comfort.

2. (An excerpt)

Lynette, you are sitting a bit higher than your mother in the picture somehow. You are holding her tightly and her arms are simply down, perhaps in her lap, but you do not notice this rather reserved posture from her. You seem almost to be taking care of her here. You look much different from most pictures with her. In this, you are not trying to move away from her, but rather pull yourself in toward her—almost like when you know a pool will be cold but you just take a deep breath and jump in, though in this case perhaps not quite as consciously.

My in-laws' home is a place of warmth and acceptance, of course from my point of view. And perhaps I so wanted to have that relationship with my mother that day, that I almost ignored the normal things that bother me and found the warmth and acceptance with her to be like the rest of the gang. But it did work.

◆

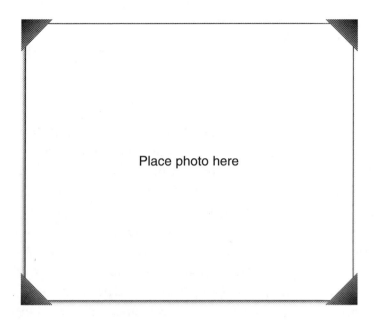

Place photo here

Answer these questions in your own mind as you look at the picture as a warm-up to the exercise or as a separate journaling exercise:

What feelings come up as you look at this picture?

What do you imagine the people (including yourself) are thinking?

What do you imagine they would like to say?

What would you like to say to yourself or to anyone else in this picture?

What does this picture mean or symbolize to you?

What part of yourself in this photo would you like to keep?

What part of yourself would you like to let go of?

What strengths do you see in yourself in this photograph?

Reverse roles with yourself in this photograph and write a monologue describing your inner experience, e.g., I am Lynette and I am feeling . . .

◆

EXERCISE 4

The Silenced Self Dialogue

Goal: Most of us try to avoid pain, and we do this in many different ways. Sometimes we actively silence that part of ourselves that would speak about our hurt and loss. In this exercise we are giving that silenced part of ourselves a voice in order to have it aid in our healing journey.

Requirements: Paper or electronic journal.

Instructions: It can be helpful to give that silent part of ourselves a name, such as Depression or Loneliness or Fear, and then allow that named part to speak. This acceptance of an unnamed and ignored part of ourselves can bring about a subtle transformation, so that it loses its tight grip on our heart and we can learn from it what we need to do to transform our life. Afterwards, write a journal entry on how it felt to do this process. Then you may speak *as* yourself today back *to* the silenced part of yourself that has just spoken. (see example below)

Sample (an excerpt):

> I am Depression in your life. As you know, I play a very big part. I come and go as I please and I know that you are trying to live without me, but don't worry. I'll always be there. I am so strong and powerful that it is very hard for you to get rid of me. In fact, I can't even imagine being wiped out altogether.
>
> Let me discuss how strong I am. I am a powerhouse. When I team up with Sadness, I am especially fierce. You are so pathetic, crying a lot . . . and you don't know why! It's because I (Depression along with my friend Sadness) come in and ruin your fun. Ya know, I don't like you to have too much

fun. I don't like you succeeding too much either. I don't even want you to have too much happiness in any area. If you ask me why that is, I guess I'd say it's because, well, WOW! . . . that's a tough question . . . I guess it's because I'm just so good at being Depression! You know me so well, and I just come in and take over. I am so very much stronger than Happiness (which must be somewhere in you). You and I are very familiar with one another. Happiness is only fleeting. HA!

You know, even when you try on that happiness feeling, I actually think I am still present. Somewhere. I get small from time to time, but it's rare that I ever completely go away. I am huge! Now I know you try to get rid of me. You take vitamins (multi- and B) and you actually think they help stamp me out a little. (I'm still there, though, deep down.) You allow your family and friends to make you very happy, but don't worry, deep down I'm still there.

Lately, you cry so much. I not only get you upset over your own life, but I also make you upset over other sad things going on in the world. Okay, even I'll admit some of this other stuff is truly sad. But I make you cry over it and let it carry over into your life! For example, when you heard about the young woman from New Jersey who died in a terrorist attack in Israel—a woman you didn't even know—you literally burst into tears! When you hear about people getting cancer (even if they're not close to you), you cry and feel this horrible sadness. When you met a dog in your elevator that was very sick, you were so sad you could hardly carry on for a few minutes. I mean, I am powerful as Depression, but accompany me with Sadness and POW! I am HERCULES!

As Depression I show myself in different ways. I used to make you tired a lot. Unfortunately, it's hard for me to show my Depressed face when you sleep. I also love to show up during PMS time. I notice I come when you are at your weakest.

I've eased up a bit, though. Since you were so affected by me and I saw how hard it was for you, I now try to only a last a few days instead of weeks (how sweet I can be!).

I mostly show up in certain situations. There are many. First of all, you think your career isn't going as planned. I know you didn't expect to be going on this way at 30 years old. You wanted more. I throw fuel on the fire and make you even more disappointed with everything. You have no healthy romantic relationship in your life. You say it isn't really that big of a deal now, but I make you afraid of never finding anyone! When you see your closest friends with their husbands, homes, furniture, future plans, and kids on the way, you feel disappointed with your own life. This is one area where I can really scare you. In fact, whenever you're upset about something and you're vulnerable, that's my clue to just jump on it! Wow! I didn't even realize up until now what a strong relationship we have.

◆

I would like to comment on what my Depression just said. I really need to point out that this exercise was very hard for me to do. I found it difficult to speak as Depression and separate it from me. It made me realize that I am not Depression. I am something else, and I just need to have more power over it. It will help me to realize that Depression and I are separate, even though we often mesh together and feel like one thing. I will now try to watch it more and notice when I'm vulnerable, and be ready to push Depression away.

I would now like to reverse roles with Depression and speak directly as myself now to this Depression. Pardon me, Depression, but just who do you think you are? You think you are so important to my life. You think I need you to survive? Well, you're wrong! In fact, I'm so tired of you! I'm sick of you! Yes, we had a long relationship. Well, I'm going to sever those ties now. Oh . . . you think you'll stick to me like glue when I'm happy or trying to be? Well, you are SO WRONG!! I am deserving of happiness. Big-time happiness! I don't need any cloud or residue from you, Depression. I guess I can thank you for your role. Maybe I needed you at one time, but that's it. I'm going to succeed whether you like it or not. You're much smaller than you think you are. I am much bigger and stronger than you! When I feel you coming on I will fight against you like an army. So long, Depression. I am working to completely wipe you out, and my goal is to push you so far out of my life that I don't even recognize you. Happiness is going to prevail.

◆

EXERCISE 5

The Somatic Dialogue

Goal: Many theorists and practitioners now believe that we can hold pain within the body. Just as you hold tension in your muscles beyond the event that caused the tension or stress, painful memories can be stored in the body through cellular memory. By allowing the body to speak through journaling, you can increase your awareness of a particular issue.

Requirements: Paper or electronic journal.

Instructions: Use your imagination to select a part of your body that may want to dialogue with you. Allow your intuition to lead you toward a part of your body that has something to say. In this exercise, you will write your journal entry as if you were that body part, speaking clearly about all that it feels and thinks.

Sample (an excerpt):

I am your leg and I feel very unwanted. You depend on me so much. You want me to carry you wherever you want to go. You wear cheap shoes that don't help me balance and yet you despise me so much. Why is that? I work hard for you.

You are ashamed of me. Constantly, I feel you pull at me and punch at me because there are parts of me you don't find attractive. You drag me to aerobics classes and I am strong for you. I am very powerful yet you hate me so much. You think of having plastic surgery done to me. How do you think that would make me feel? What is so terrible about me? I am so strong. I work so hard. It hurts me that you hate me so much. I keep trying and trying but you just won't accept me. I am part of you. Why does that have to be so awful? Maybe I am not perfect, but neither are you. What I am is efficient and strong.

What would I have to do to have you accept me? I love you. I want you to be proud of me and accept me as part of your body. No, think of me as beautiful. I think my calves are very beautiful. The muscles are shaped and defined. My thighs are round and strong. Please love me for that. I will work with you. I will not let you down if you take care of me. I like to do aerobics, but I don't want you to hide me anymore. I don't want you to punch me in frustration anymore. I don't want you to even think about plastic surgery. I am a part of you, a valuable part. Please don't buy into some picture of what you think I should be. I am what I am. What I am is strong and beautiful. I love you. Please try to love me, too.

◆

EXERCISE 6

The Wounded Self Dialogue

Goal: To discern some wound in yourself that gets triggered by certain emotional incidents. Finding and relating to this unresolved or unhealed wounded part of yourself can lead you to a more balanced and integrated experience of this hurt. In this way, you can lessen those intense emotional reactions when this wound is touched by some slight or incident.

Requirements: Paper or electronic journal.

Instructions: First reflect on that part of you that reacts very strongly to emotional triggers—for example, if you feel like you hate it when something happens, or when you see some trait in another that makes you particularly uncomfortable. It could also be a dialogue between a wounded inner child self and you as an adult. Then, in your journal, give that wounded part a voice. And then dialogue with it and see if it has something to tell you. Include in your journal dialogue some conversation about why you don't listen to this part of yourself.

Sample (an excerpt):

> **Alix (child):** I am in the sixth grade and my teacher, Mr. Booth, just said something to me that really hurt my feelings, and he didn't even seem to care. He is my chorus teacher and I am very devoted to the class. I am sort of a good singer, but I don't get any credit for that. Anyway, my sister is in the high school chorus and she told Mr. B that I am a blimp. She called me Blimp Jones . . . or maybe that is what he called me. He told the whole sixth-grade chorus that I have a nickname my sister calls me. He said that "BJ" was short for the name. I had no idea what he was talking about and that surprised

him. He then said, "You can come up here after class and then I will tell you." So I went up to him after class and he told me what she said. I couldn't believe it.

Alix (adult): To this day I still can't believe it. I was so mad at my sister at the time but I was even more crushed by my teacher. He really was a miserable person at the time; maybe he wanted to spread his misery around.

Alix (child): I should have told him to shut up. It was all I could do to keep myself from crying, right then and there.

Alix (adult): Yes, he deserved to hear you say "shut up." That was such a horrible thing to say to you. You would think that a grown man would be able to see how hurtful something like that would be to a sixth-grade girl. That really must have hurt you.

Alix (child): It did hurt me—not only that he told me, but that he was ready to humiliate me in front of the class. It is like he despised me or something. I knew my sister hated me, but that really hurt. She said mean things about me to my teacher, a man I respected. I didn't realize how much I grossed her out and embarrassed her.

(This dialogue continues with an even fuller expression of feeling and hurt and woundedness. This incident in class symbolized and led into other issues around body image and Alix's relationship with her sister.)

◆

EXERCISE 7

The Shadow Self Dialogue

Goal: To interact with that part of our self that we keep hidden, that part of our self that we reject and say is not really who we are. This aspect or "shadow" dimension of our personality is often buried in our unconscious and is hard for us to acknowledge, even hard for us to admit that it exists or is a part of us. By interacting with this "shadow" self, we can begin to bring rejected parts of ourselves up to consciousness and embrace them as parts of our total self.

Requirements: Paper or electronic journal.

Instructions: Giving voice to our "shadow" is one of the most demanding of all dialogues. It requires courageous self-honesty and persistence. So think about the feelings that you are most uncomfortable with as a starting point. If anger was not expressed in your family, it may very well be that you have anger in your "shadow." Or it may be that you are very "nice" in real life, and therefore you have a "shadow" that longs to express contrary feelings and to tell some people strong negative things that are not nice. Speak freely; allow the shadow within you to have a voice.

Sample (an excerpt):

Liza: Shadow? Hi, I know you're never very far from the surface. You are definitely a stubborn and strong shadow. Sometimes I really hate you and your persistent existence; other times I can't imagine life without you.

Shadow: Well, you can't lose me, detach me or even kill me. But you know that; you've thought about this a lot.

Liza: I think you're the biggest part of me, the negative, fearful, closed-off Liza. The almost always present depression, negativity and cynicism that I know are ugly emotions and ones other people don't want to hear or deal with. I used to tell myself all the time how boring and depressing I must appear, how distasteful to be with. I'm a little better now, I think . . .

Shadow: Deep down you believe in predetermination. No matter how hard you might want to fight your inner make-up, you won't win. It's there, indelibly imprinted and forever with you. So just accept it and stop the torment.

Liza: Am I better? Have I changed at all? Would I give you up if it were possible? I know I want to lighten up; I would love to be more trusting and self-affirming. I try not to be so serious all the time, so easily affected and moody, I really do! It scares me that I often feel programmed and conditioned to act and react certain ways. Those ways are too much like my father (and we all know what's happened to him).

Shadow: You're boring me.

Liza: I bore me. I disgust me. I would gladly rip my brain open and vomit up all this dreck and grime. I want out. I want to swim, not just feel as though I'm treading water. I have passion, I have insight, I have a good heart. I know that and I want to use it all better.

Shadow: You're quite emotional today.

Liza: And you're destructive, scared and egotistical. You get a perverse kick out of being alienated and constantly in a state of flux.

Shadow: Come on, a part of you enjoys your many contradictions. Admit it.

Liza: Okay, some of them, yes. They can be quirky and surprising, even exciting. But they can also be harmful and hurtful. Sometimes even self-defeating and perpetually setting me up for disappointment, too.

Shadow: And part of you recognizes that a lot of this "dreck" was developed—well developed! It was done in order that you would survive. You are a survivor, and mainly because of me.

Liza: But I don't need you so much now. I gave birth to you and needed you most when I was a teenager. That lost thing, that screwed-up thing that only felt miserable most of the time. I am stronger now. I've dealt with a lot and you have helped there, I must admit. I just don't want to be walled up so much of the time any more. I'd at least like to give it a go with a little less of you intruding. You'll always be there if I need some more support and protection, right? Take a little time off. You deserve it; you've worked hard for a very long time.

Shadow: Trying to charm me, are you? It's not that easy. Still, I'll do some cognitive processing and get back to you. Try not to be too cheerful, though, sweetie—it doesn't really suit you.

◆

EXERCISE 8

A Dream Dialogue

Goal: To understand a dream, to find out what it might be telling us about ourselves that is relevant to our journey of grief and healing. Dreams have long been seen as a doorway to the unconscious. They carry in them our personalized system of metaphor and symbol, and thus are significant as stories about our emotional lives. More accurately, they are internal pictures of how we experience the world. They describe to us the contents of our unconscious and are revelatory in the sense that they describe it as we ourselves see it. Consciously we may try to deny to ourselves how we feel, but our unconscious is constantly attempting to messenger that information to our conscious mind. It is my observation that even our unconscious has governors and delivers information as we can cope with it. In other words, it obscures meaning that is overwhelming for us. Dreams offer us a window through which we can peer into our personalized representation of our own inner world.

Requirements: Paper or electronic journal (you might even consider starting a separate dream journal).

Instructions: Write down a dream in your journal. The most helpful way is to separate the page in half vertically or horizontally with a line and write the dream on one side or above the line, leaving the other portion blank. Then on the blank side you can write down your associations, feelings and thoughts about the dream. Remember, most dreams are describing the contents of our unconscious, not what is happening in the external world, even though it may use people, places and events from the external world in a symbolic way.

Samples:

Example One: This was a dream that occurred a couple of years before Dan's mother died.

Dream:

I was inside a wooden house, small, run-down, a bit ramshackle, and an elephant appeared on the large porch. I could see it coming up onto the porch until it filled the doorway and the windows with its size and its color. Before the elephant sat down on the porch it defecated right there. Then it sat down on the porch and the whole house shook. Just as I was waking up the elephant's face began to shift into my mother's face. It was very disturbing.

Reflections:

The house felt like me, and I felt shaky right about that time, struggling with work and with relationships and with single-parenting. The large gray presence that was my mother felt suffocating and a bit dangerous. Her presence was not wanted in my unconscious. It was an unwanted and inappropriate figure to be on my porch. Somehow I needed to rid myself of this large gray presence that was leaving unwanted waste in my life, and to live with the loss of my interior mother presence.

Example Two: Lee is a student in the United States whose family is in the Far East. Her sister is getting married.

Dream:

I dreamt that my sister and I were in a shopping mall and we went down the escalator. Then there was a ledge we could sit on and there was this huge billowing cloth that was on the ledge and covered the rest of the space to our right. This cloth was moving as if in the wind, and when we sat on the ledge we were pushed by this cloth just like waves push us when we sit at the beach. A male security guard was watching us. My sister's shoe fell from her foot, rose up in the air, then fell on the cloth. I kept thinking, I'm leaving for the States again in a few hours and I have to say good-bye to my family.

Reflections: (Below is Lee's own analysis of her dream, which she later turned into a painting): . . .

I woke up with this dream and I remembered all the dreams I used to have every night about desperately wanting to be with my family. It felt like my mind refused to acknowledge the reality of space and time. In my dreams, my family's home is just around the corner from where I live.

I remembered my sister's wedding and maybe some part of me did not want her to be married. I noticed the man looking at us and I said to myself, "He's spoiling our fun." Was he our dad? I think he's more likely her husband. Is there some sort of Cinderella thing there (dropping a shoe)? I definitely did not think he should catch that shoe. Maybe I'm thinking about my own wedding or if I really wanted to get married. The reality is, our lives are limited to what kind of husband we marry. Self-determination and career for women—yes, they are there. But at the same time, marriage is a compromise and your opportunities are limited to what your husband's opportunities are. If my sister did not have a boyfriend, she would be here right now, following me where I go, looking for a residency program (she's a medical school graduate). And of course, I'd feel very insecure about that.

◆

EXERCISE 9

The Letter-Writing Experience

Goal: This letter is not being sent to anyone. It is an attempt to say what you may have always wanted or needed to say to someone about unresolved feelings.

Requirements: Paper or electronic journal.

Instructions: Pick someone that you need to express feelings to. Write out your feelings in the form of a letter with a greeting (Dear Dad) and don't hold back. Or you may want to write a letter that you would have liked to *receive*. In that case, write the letter as if you were the person expressing feelings to you that you wanted and needed to hear as a corrective experience.

Sample: Here is an example of Jack's letter to his father and his wished-for response. Jack lost his father as a baby. He lives daily with the father he never had the opportunity to know. In his process page letter, he reaches out to touch the father who has been a ghost in his life. Then, he reverses roles with his father and writes the words he has longed for 54 years to hear.

Dear Dad,

My God how I long to know you. Funny, the word "dad" sounds odd. I've never even called anyone "dad" in my life. Dad, Daddy, Father, Pa, Pop, my old man—how I long to feel your strength envelop my body. How I wish I could have known you, met you, touched you, kissed you, fought with you and deeply loved you.

I've never, ever heard you speak, yell, tell me to go to bed, do my homework and don't answer my mother back. Don't fight with your brothers and sisters. I've never heard you say, "Let's go up to Maine to visit Grandpa and all your aunts and uncles. We'll have a great time fishing, swimming, canoeing on Moosehead Lake." When I really did go up to Maine to visit Grandpa and all my aunts and uncles, you weren't there, and they treated me like a stranger. I met you once in a psychodrama. A man named Lyle played you in a role. He and I have become good friends. Thanks for speaking to me through him.

Love from your son, Jack

Dear Son,

My heart aches that I had to die and leave your mom with four of my children, and how it grieves me to have missed the golden opportunity to see you come into this world. Jacko, I'm so proud of you for all your accomplishments and for what a fine man you've turned out to be. A good husband, stepfather and a real great grandfather. I'll always be near to you. All you have to do is think of me and I'll always be close in your imagination to guide you.

With all my love, Dad

◆

EXERCISE 10

The Learning-by-Imitation Monologue

Goal: To help us learn what we do in our relationships that we *imitate* or model from what we saw in the intimate relationships that surrounded us when we were growing up.

Requirements: Paper or electronic journal.

Instructions: This exercise is a simple question/answer journal-writing experience. Remember, relationships get sick in parts. A relationship can have a very sick dynamic of dysfunctional rather than healthy fighting, for example, and still remain fairly stable and happy in other areas. The more accurately we can learn to see where the relationship is sick, the more we can focus energy toward repairing and rebuilding that area before it contaminates other parts of the relationship. We learn relationship lessons not only from how we were treated by parents or caregivers and siblings, but by what we saw. How did those significant adults during our growing-up years conduct their own intimate relationship, and what did we learn by watching them and being a child in the atmosphere of their particular intimacy dynamic?

Questions:

1. Spend a few moments reflecting on the primary caregiving relationship from your childhood, whether it was close or distant. In the case of divorce, you may have observed your parents' divorced relationship as well as a stepparent relationship. You may wish to use photographs to stimulate memories.

2. Ask yourself these questions: How did my parents or caregivers express love? What was the feeling atmosphere

around those relationships? How did they handle conflict? How did they express their sexuality?

3. What did I learn about relationships and intimacy from my parents or caregivers?

4. If my parents' relationship had a voice, what would it have said?

5. How has what I learned impacted or been played out in my intimate relationships?

Sample: This excerpt is just entitled Imitation, and it conveys what a person might think about when reflecting on the model provided in early years for relationship.

Reflecting on my parents' "relationship" leaves me with empty images. They separated when I was two years old, so as far as I'm concerned, they were never really together. I don't remember them as a couple, and I don't remember my father occupying our house. Photographs of my parents from the past seem false, as if they had posed for the pictures so that they would eventually have proof—proof of something that never really existed. I learned the word "divorce" when I was six years old—the day my dad showed me the official divorce papers. Although I had never witnessed my parents as a couple, there was a harsh reality to face upon seeing documents stating that the marriage between my parents was legally ended. Until that moment, somewhere in my heart there was always hope that my parents would be a couple again. For them, I am sure it was a sigh of relief. For me, as a small child, it was a slap in the face, an unchangeable truth and a lost hope.

I have no memory of my parents expressing love for each other. The feeling atmosphere around their relationship was conflict. Conflict and fighting. How did they handle conflict? They used a reliable scapegoat—money. Everything was about money. Money Money Money. Of course, other problems arose over the years, but the majority of the fighting was over money matters. Petty and silly. Stupid and safe.

If my parents' relationship had a voice, what would it have said? It would have said: "I'm sorry . . . . I'm sorry that you don't believe I was ever good. I'm sorry you didn't get to know my good side better. I'm sorry you only saw me when I had turned sour. I wish you could have seen me when we laughed together, traveled together, embraced each other and loved each other.

"I'm sorry that you have to sit here today writing about me as a painful memory. I'm sorry that I did not have better gifts to leave with you. I'm sorry that you are crying as you write this. I'm sorry that I couldn't set a better example for you and your future relationships. I'm sorry that I inspired you to have a money panic that consumes you so often. I'm sorry I caused you to feel so isolated from your friends, who all had parents that were married. I'm sorry, so, so sorry, that your father leaving left the door open for later traumatic situations at home. But as the voice of your parents' relationship, I also have the responsibility of checking in with you in the present. I need to remind you that the conflict has been replaced with friendship. My role as relationship has been magically transformed into something positive rather than negative. You are lucky that the fighting has ceased. But I also cannot deny that the old wounds run deep, and there is no way to change the past."

The lessons I learned about relationships and intimacy from my parents have only recently become more clear. Obviously, they were not exemplary role models in the love department. I learned that love can fail, that it can end, and that "living happily ever after" is not guaranteed when two people fall in love. I learned to fear relationships, intimate relationships, and approached them with caution—yet I desperately craved them. Relationships and intimacy were mysterious to me, since I had never witnessed either between my parents firsthand.

It is difficult to make a clear distinction between what I learned from my parents about relationships and how it has made an impact on me in my relationships. I think that a lot of what I learned from my parents' relationship was tucked away in my subconscious, so that only when I started to pursue my own relationships did these "lessons" surface. Even now I am in the process of trying to understand and make conscious some of these stored fears about relationships. Perhaps that is the key to the feeling of mysteriousness behind relationships for me—my parents did not provide me with lessons on love, but rather fears, and it is quite common to fear the unknown.

◆

EXERCISE 11

Understanding Projections

Goal: To understand through a writing exercise how a past hurt or wound can be seen in the present, through a process called projection.

Requirements: Paper or electronic journal.

Instructions: First, take some time to reflect on the definition of "projection." A projection is a transference. It is the transferring of an unconscious feeling or pattern of feelings onto another person. Often the intensity of the unconscious feeling or pattern of feelings is transferred also. For example, you might secretly or unconsciously despise your own obesity, but instead of admitting that to yourself because it is so painful to acknowledge, you transfer that set of feelings or feeling onto your mother and say that she despises your obesity. And you might even make that more intense by saying that she must despise you as a person because of the obesity. The truth may be that she is concerned and it causes her some anxiety, but she does not despise it, nor does she despise you. These kinds of projections are very difficult to acknowledge and stop.

Second, write down the name of someone who annoys you or causes you pain and describe what it is that annoys you or hurts you. Take time to describe this person's behavior or attitudes and how they affect you.

Third, ask yourself if you have ever acted in a similar way or exhibited a similar attitude, and briefly describe.

Sample:

1. I find that I have intense feelings around authority figures in my life. And those feelings seem stronger than whatever

that authority figure might actually do that irritates me in any certain situation.

2. I work with a man named Jake who is very bossy. He treats me as if I don't know what I am doing and is always checking up on me. He is not my boss, but he acts like he is and it makes me very angry. His bossiness and "steamroller" personality really grate on me.

3. In some consulting situations with younger colleagues I can be arrogant and bossy. They have finally told me this and it was very upsetting. I probably don't like Jake's attitudes or behavior because they are so much like my own. And now that I think about it, my dad was extremely bossy and never had a conversation about anything; he just told me what to do and got angry if I didn't do it his way. And he would fly into a rage at the smallest infraction, and scared all of us siblings because he seemed so out of control.

◆

EXERCISE 12

Linking Understanding, Beliefs and Perceptions

Goal: To understand what beliefs and perceptions about ourselves that we associated with a trauma, loss or hurt from the past.

Requirements: Paper or electronic journal.

Instructions: A trauma or hurt or loss from the past can cause us to believe something about ourselves that is somewhat distorted. The younger we were at the time of trauma, the more distorted this belief might be. For example, young children who are abused often believe that they must be "bad" people or the wiser, stronger adult would not have hurt them. That belief in their "badness" can affect their sense of self-esteem throughout their lives. This belief or perception that is distorted can have a life of its own. It then might influence our patterns of both how we see ourselves and how we experience relationships. This is how the past gets played out in our present-day lives, mixing up unresolved pain from an original wound into a behavior or belief that is operational in relationships. So take some time to reflect on the following questions, fill in the information requested, and then connect the distorted belief or perception to the relationship where it is most obviously acted out.

Sample:

1. Choose a wound or hurt from the past and write a brief paragraph about that experience and how it made you feel.

   Example: My dad and mom divorced when I was 12, and my mom left me with my dad and went off with another man. I started cleaning, cooking and taking care of my dad even though I was really angry and confused that my mom left me.

2. List the feelings you experienced around the loss or trauma.

    a. Worry and anxiety

    b. A sense of feeling left behind

    c. Helplessness

3. List the perceptions or beliefs that you learned from that experience.

    a. If I don't take care of a man, he will leave me.

    b. Women are unreliable and will leave you even when you don't want them to, and even though they said they wouldn't.

    c. There must be something wrong with me if my mom didn't want me.

4. List the relationships in which you act out that belief or perception.

    a. I have trouble trusting. I feel that if I love a woman she might leave me.

    b. I sometimes have a difficult time with boundaries in my friendships with women.

    c. I tend to get overly anxious when my children have problems.

    d. Moments of intense closeness make me anxious and want to argue or distance myself.

    e. When my wife is away for even two days I can feel very abandoned.

◆

Linking Understanding, Beliefs and Perceptions

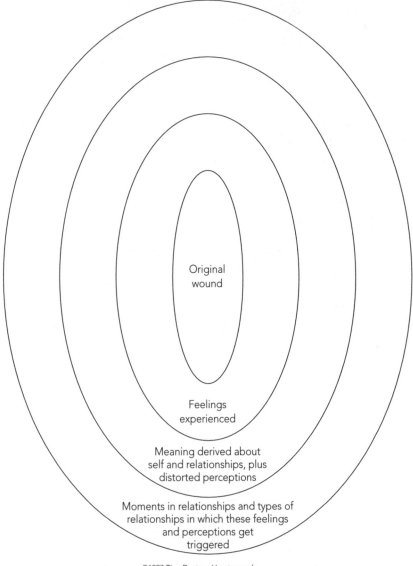

Original
wound

Feelings
experienced

Meaning derived about
self and relationships, plus
distorted perceptions

Moments in relationships and types of
relationships in which these feelings
and perceptions get
triggered

©1997 Tian Dayton, *Heartwounds*

EXERCISE 13

Writing Your Own Story

Goal: An exercise to help each of us understand how certain past experiences can shape our lives today.

Requirements: Paper or electronic journal.

Instructions: Choose a period in your life that was painful and helped shape who you are today. Then write a story in the first or third person that describes the situation. Be sure to include the surrounding circumstances and the emotional climate of both your inner thoughts and feelings and the outer events.

Sample (an excerpt from Amanda):

I abused drugs and alcohol to help change my reality—to alter my perceptions. I wanted transcendence. Now I think that I had the right idea, just the wrong means of getting there. I always wanted to be closer to God in a way. I used marijuana so that everything would be beautiful. I was beautiful. Life was a big tea party and I was the star attraction. It worked for a long time. I felt like it was saving my life. I was self-medicating so that I didn't have to go on Prozac (as I flippantly told my therapists on many occasions). I was the party girl, the happy girl. I showed the person that was a sure thing—the one everybody liked—because I'm afraid that I'll never be loved for who I am. Yet at the same time, I'm afraid of experiencing real love because I'm not sure what it is. . . . I've often felt that my experience with men and relationships was like a battering of my head against a wall. I longed to break through it, but until I brought to consciousness some reasons for this pattern of behavior, I was doomed to repeat it. I always sought out men who were emotionally unavailable.

And if they were available, I didn't want them, because part of my inner reality was that I would never be loved.

I've had many short, intensely sexual affairs with men that I was obsessed with. My role in these "relationships" was the "sex object"; I totally sexualized myself and played the role that I thought these men wanted. The role I thought that would get them to fall madly in love with me. And these men were all interchangeable. I could fall "in love" with anyone. And I would always have the sensation of falling, that there was not something quite right. I felt so empty and so uncomfortable with myself that I constantly sought to fill the hole. Fortunately, I never got myself into an abusive long-term relationship, but as we shall see, my heart always really belonged to Daddy anyway.

I am exploring the possibility that this hunger comes from the need to complete my relationship with my father, whom I both intensely idolized and feared. He is wonderful and charismatic, yet tortured and inconsistent. He loved me. I was his princess, yet he was never really emotionally available for me while I was growing up. There was nobody I loved or feared more. Consequently, these two emotions have overlapped in my search for a partner. I have sought out the victim role with men because it was my reality. I placed myself in dangerous situations: I was molested as a preteen and raped at the age of 22. I pause on the page, as I am at a loss for words. It is amazing to me how much the man who raped me reminded me of my father, and how he justified his violence toward me because I was "bad," and this man raped me because I was "bad." Both experiences were horrible and violent, and all the more confusing because both cases were people that I knew and trusted. Was the rape a repetition of my early relationship with Daddy? It's certainly a great example of how we remain stuck until we can find the help and the strength to question. It's hard to write about my father in a negative way because my relationship with him has changed so much; he is still my favorite person in the whole world.

◆

EXERCISE 14

A Personal Time Line

Goal: To understand our personal history of loss and trauma, to illuminate the cumulative nature of trauma.

Requirements: Paper or electronic journal. The trauma time line chart.

Instructions: Using the chart provided, reflect on the overall patterns of loss and trauma as they have occurred in your life.

Sample: Using words or phrases, write losses or traumas in the appropriate year space on your time line that corresponds to your life. Next, reflect on these questions as you look at your time line:

- What new awarenesses do you have when you look at your filled-in time line?
- Are there particular periods where loss and/or trauma pile up?
- Are there some traumas that are sustained over a long period of time?
- Can you identify areas where traumatic childhood dynamics were reenacted or re-created in later years?
- Which losses and traumas feel resolved, and which ones feel unresolved?

◆

Birth Through 80 Years

0	5	10	15	20
				moved cities
				changed schools
			two other siblings	grandmother died
	mother's alcoholism began to take hold	parents' divorce	leave for college	graduated college

30	35	40	45	50
		my divorce		mother died
		job change	downsizing—	first child went to college
	husband's alcoholism got bad	moved cities	lost job, moved cities for new job	second child went to college
married husband	second child	got MBA		
first child		remarried		
		blended families		

60	65	70	75	80
			retired	
		daughter divorced	sister got lupus	husband died
husband got cancer	sister got divorced			

Your Personal Time Line

| 0 | 5 | 10 | 15 | 20 |

| 30 | 35 | 40 | 45 | 50 |

| 60 | 65 | 70 | 75 | 80 |

Create your own time line by filling in words in the appropriate spaces that express any trauma or loss that you have experienced.

EXERCISE 15

An Empowerment
Life Episode Monologue

Goal: To understand our own experiences of feeling empowered and how we can access those feelings today and learn from them.

Requirements: Paper or electronic journal.

Instructions: Think of a time in your life when you felt very empowered. Write a story or journal entry as that person, as if it were the here and now. Then write a reflection on your monologue from your perspective today.

Sample (an excerpt):

It's a beautiful day. The air is so fresh in my nose that it hurts. I can smell the pine trees and the grass heating up in the sun. I can smell the dew evaporating off the leaves and blades of grass. It smells so fresh! I can smell the water in the lake beyond the trees. I can smell the mud. I can hear birds singing.

I am 15 and I am riding a pony. She is too small for me really, but she needed some exercise and I am the only one who wanted to help my friend out. I have two horses of my own. My big Appaloosa, Apollo, is at home, no doubt enjoying the sun also. And Dixie, my quarter horse Arabian mare, is at the stable. This pony is a friend's. She hasn't ridden Queenie in a while, and Queenie is starting to get too fat. She is tan, with black legs and face. In the middle of her forehead is a star. She smells very strong. I don't mind. I love the smell of horses. She needs a bath, though. And a good grooming. I decide I will do that after our ride. I am riding her bareback.

My legs are warm around her fat little sides as we trot along. She is already breathing a bit heavily. I pull her in and let her walk slowly down the trail.

We are in Beaver Lake Park. This park is very big and has many trails and fields for riders to use. Beaver Lake is in the middle of the park, and it connects to another lake named Elk Lake. The two parks are connected by what's called the Pipeline Trail. We just call it the Pipeline. The park has huge meadows that everyone rides their horses through. It is a great place to be on a sunny spring day. Riding Queenie reminds me of my first pony, Star. He was such a brat. He sure taught me how to ride. He used to bite my toes, and buck me off and run home, and all sorts of things. I loved him so much. Today, I miss him. Queenie, the fat little thing, reminds me of him. Her owner and I used to run on these trails, when I had Star, and Queenie wasn't fat and forgotten. Queenie was her owner's passing phase. Now she doesn't stand a chance against boyfriends. Poor thing. I pat her neck. She perks up a bit and starts to walk a bit faster. I wonder what she's thinking. I wonder if she misses the days we used to run on these trails together.

I start to sing under my breath, and Queenie's ears flick back at me. She slows down, listening. I start to sing songs from the musical *Oliver!* I love that musical. I start to really belt them out, really loud, singing at the top of my lungs "Food, glorious, food!" and Queenie starts to flick her ears back and forth, and she starts to trot and I'm singing, and she's trotting down the trail, past the lake, past the empty changing rooms, past the public bathrooms, down another trail toward the fields. I am singing, and the sun is so warm and I feel like a kid again. I feel like I'm on Star again and I am nine years old and I don't have to ever worry about exams and school and theater stuff, and auditions. It's all lifted off my shoulders. And that's how we are when around the corner comes another riding party. I stop singing, and Queenie stops dead in her tracks. I start to laugh. I can't help it. It's like Queenie was more embarrassed than I was. They pass us by, silently, trying to hide their smiles at us. Fat little Queenie with her oversized rider, bareback, slogging down the muddy, spring trails. I'm sure we look funny.

I don't sing the rest of the way home. Inside I am completely warm. I feel like Queenie and I shared something profound. I do not sing because it would have been like trying to regain the moment before. The present was perfect enough. It was enough to ride home and enjoy the sounds of the park around us and the heat of the sun on our faces. I give Queenie a bath and a brush and a lot of hugs. I don't think I will ever forget this day.

This exercise was saddening for me. I remembered the day so clearly, and it felt like I was there again. I felt a longing to be in that place again. I love animals and horses in particular, and I miss the West Coast so much it brings up the sadness of leaving my old friends again. That's what my horses were to me. They were my very best friends most of the time. I used to run down to the barn every morning and evening to take care of them and be with them. I used to spend whole weekends riding. I would come home from school and hang out in the barn. Cleaning them, feeding them, grooming them, talking to them, being with them. This was a very powerful time regression.

◆

EXERCISE 16

Letter to God

Goal: To increase your sense of God's presence in your life and to help you have faith that God might help you.

Requirements: Paper or electronic journal.

Instructions: This is a straight writing assignment that is meant to help you express your feelings about God or a Higher Power, and to help you open yourself to something good happening. So pick a current situation in your life that seems in need of help. Describe that situation in a paragraph. Then describe how you would like for that circumstance or situation to be. When describing it, do so as if it was actually happening as if the experience was real. Finally, leave a blank space where you can imagine divine help entering and working.

1. (Bottom third of the paper) Describe the situation as it now exists.

    Recently I met someone who seems like a very possible life partner, but this person lives many states away. The distance creates a lot of frustration, including some anger at myself for allowing this to happen. I am also aware that I am angry at God because it seems as if I will never be happy in an intimate relationship, and this is just one more example of why it won't happen.

2. (Top third of the paper) Describe how you wish this circumstance might be.

    We are living together happily in a committed relationship. We talk over problems openly as they arise in a vulnerable, supportive manner. We are in love and feel deeply

connected. We have fun together and enjoy the little pleasures of life as a couple.

3. (Middle of the paper) Divine Work, enter here!

◆

Letter to God Sample Chart

We are living together happily in a committed relationship. We talk over problems openly as they arise in a vulnerable, supportive manner. We are in love and feel deeply connected. . . .

How I wish this circumstance might be

Divine Work Enter Here!

Space for God to enter and work

Recently I met someone who seems like a very possible life partner, but this person lives many states away. The distance causes a lot of frustration, including some anger at myself for allowing this to happen. . . .

The situation as it exists now

Letter to God Chart

Divide the page into three parts. In the bottom third, write a few phrases that describe a current situation that you would like to transform and heal. In the top third, write a few phrases that describe how you wish this situation might be. Leave the middle section empty for God to enter and work.

How I wish this circumstance might be

Space for God to enter and work

The situation as it exists now

✦ APPENDIX ✦

his section is a study guide for professionals and affiliated lay people working with issues of grief and mourning. The exercises may be used in:

1. Grief groups
2. Therapy groups
3. Support groups
4. Religious-based groups

Overall Focus

When we lose a person, whether to death, divorce, addiction, mental illness or alienation, we are left with a vague and free-floating sense of loss. Words that were not spoken, anger and love that went unexpressed, and feelings that went unshared need to be brought out into the open, shared or concretized so that they can be felt, understood and reintegrated with today's perspective. Depending upon the focus of the group and the orientation of the leader, these exercises can be adopted for clinical use in a wide variety of grief-oriented groups.

Specific Exercises

1. **Empty-Chair Work:** Using an empty chair to represent the person he or she has lost gives the grieving person the opportunity to talk to rather than about the person, saying what needs to be said, bringing thoughts and words from an unspoken state into a spoken one. Oftentimes, mourners are haunted by what they never had a chance to say and this exercise can help to bring about catharsis and therefore closure to that pain.

2. **Photographs:** Group members can bring in photographs of a person. Any photo that brings up feelings related to a loss for the mourner is fine; it is entirely the mourner's choice. Who feels lost to them or images representing a time of life that one regrets losing. The mourner can simply describe the picture to the group and share thoughts and feelings in a supportive, accepting atmosphere. The mourner can also talk directly to the picture—to a particular person in the picture or to themselves at a particular stage of life, using an empty chair to represent any one of these possibilities depending upon what the picture represents. This can create a direct connection with what the picture represents. After going through this process, it is useful to ask the mourner to share how he or she "wishes it had been." This is often a very painful moment because it puts the mourner in touch with all that was lost.

3. **Meaningful Objects:** Objects often carry deep meaning for the mourner and can bring depth and reality to the mourning process: "The chair my father sat in," "My mother's address book," "Music my sister and I shared," "A painting I bought with my husband," or "The stuffed animal my child held," are all possible examples of objects that can help one make the transition from inner to outer grief. The mourner can bring an object or a picture of the object to the group and share the experience with the others, or instead talk directly to the object

itself. He or she may even reverse roles and speak as the object back to themselves if it seems useful.

4. **Letter Writing:** Following the instructions for the letter writing exercise in section V, this exercise can be done in a grief group as well as individually. Soft background music can aid in focusing. The letter can be read to an empty chair representing the lost person or part of self. Another option is to have the letter writer choose another group member to represent the recipient of the letter. In the case where one is writing a letter they wish to receive, a role player can read the letter to the letter writer.

Group Integration

After each of these exercises, other group members should be invited to share ways in which they identify with the mourner as well as feelings that came up for them as they watched and listened. For further information on Experiential Therapy, consult *The Drama Within: Psychodrama and Experiential Therapy* by Tian Dayton, Ph.D., T.E.P., Health Communications, 1994.

Exercises in Section V and Their Application

In recovering from the trauma of loss, it is necessary to engage in a process of grief and mourning so that the issues surrounding the loss can be made conscious, felt and worked through, and placed in the perspective of one's overall life. Factors that affect one's life pattern as well as the severity of the impact of the loss can be explored in the "Grief Questionnaire." The "Time Line" can help the griever to understand patterns of loss or incomplete mourning that might be affecting his or her current experience of loss. The "Loss Chart" can help the griever to understand how a current life loss may resonate with or be complicated by previous losses. Exercises such as "The Silenced Self," "The Somatic Dialogue," "The Wounded Self Dialogue," "The Shadow Self Dialogue," and "A Dream Dialogue" offer ways to explore the personal meaning and ramifications of losses and can give voice to the parts of self that have been silenced, run from or repressed. Intergenerational pain can be explored in "The Learning-by-Imitation Monologue" so that the mourners can find out if they are living out or carrying other people's historical pain in their own lives.

Ways in which unresolved pain is being projected onto current relationships can be further understood by doing the exercise "Understanding Projections." "Linking: Understanding Beliefs and Perceptions" can help the mourner to link current problematic behavior with unresolved trauma and pain from the past.

"Writing Your Own Story" offers the mourner an opportunity to tell the story and have it witnessed by writing the story either in the group or as homework. Then it can be read to the group. "An Empowerment Life Episode Monologue" is designed to help the mourner to identify personal strength so that he or she can begin to rebuild in a positive way. And the "Letter to God" opens the heart to receive spiritual guidance. In religious or spiritually oriented groups, the leader can introduce the idea of intergenerational prayer, praying for all generations past, present and future to be released from the grip of intergenerational family pain, and also praying that pain enrich and bear wisdom rather than debilitate and destroy.

For an overall map of the process reread section V: "Personal Journey." It expands on these stages (1) Acknowledge the Loss, (2) Tell the Story and Bear Witness, (3) Linking, (4) Separating the Past from the Present, and (5) Creating a New Narrative and Finding Meaning.

Some Hints

Any of these exercises can be used in the group as homework or as a warm-up to experiential work. In the case of experiential work, however, it is best to have a professional who is trained in leading it. When no leader is present, such as in "Personal Journaling," leaderless support groups or 12-Step work, stay within your comfort zone in choosing which exercises to do. In such cases, avoid analyzing other people's experience, cross-talk and advice giving. Simply do the exercises and share them in a supportive atmosphere.

In all groups end each exercise with sharing, giving each group member the opportunity for closure, identification and healing of the feelings that are brought up for them in the witness or audience role.

Healing from trauma through a process of mourning is both a painful and a transformative experience. It puts us in touch both with the agony and the ecstasy of life and carries within it a dialogue with the divine and a drive to integrate the opposing and paradoxical side of the human experience. These exercises are a simple architecture that are brought to life and given depth and beauty over and over again in unique ways by the beauty and wisdom of each individual's heart and mind.

◆ REFERENCES ◆

Aleyden, S. (1997). *The Knitting Sutra*. San Francisco: Harper.

Allen, J. Ph.D. (1996). "The Renfew Perspective," Summer, 2(2).

Benson, H. (1996) (with Marg Stark). *Timeless Healing: The Power and Biology of Belief*. New York: Scribner.

Bowlby, J. (1973). *Attachment and Loss*, Vol. I *Attachment*. New York: Basic Books.

———— (1973). *Attachment and Loss*, Vol. II. *Separation, Anxiety and Anger*. New York: Basic Books.

———— (1980). *Attachment and Loss*, Vol. III: *Loss, Sadness and Depression*. New York: Basic Books.

Butler, K. (1997). "The Anatomy of Resilience," *The Networker*, March/April, p. 25.

Campbell, J. and Moyers, B. (1988). *The Power of Myth*. New York: Doubleday.

Carpi, J. (1996). "A Smorgasbord of Stress-Stoppers," *Psychology Today*, Jan./Feb.

Czikszentmilahyi, M. (1990). *Flow: The Psychology of Optimal Experience*. New York: HarperCollins Publishers.

Danieli, Y. (1984). "Psychotherapists' Participation in the Conspiracy of Silence About the Holocaust," *Psychoanalytic Psychology*, p. 23-42.

Dawson, J. (1993) "Deep in the Human Mind," *Minneapolis Star-Tribune,* May.

Dreher, H. (1995). *The Immune Power Personality.* New York: NAL Dutton.

Driver, T. F. (1991). *The Magic of Ritual: Our Need for Liberating Rites That Transform Our Lives and Our Communities.* New York: HarperCollins.

Ferguson, E., Howell, M. (1994). "Focusing," *Medical Self-Care,* Summer, 57-59.

Fox, M. & Sheldrake, R. (1996). *Natural Grace: Dialogues on Creation, Darkness, and the Soul in Spirituality and Science.* New York: Doubleday.

Erikson, Joan M. (1988). *Wisdom and the Senses: The Way to Creativity.* New York: W.W. Norton & Co.

Green, B. L., Grace, J. D., et al. (1990). "Risk Factors for PTSD and Other Diagnoses in a General Sample of Vietnam Veterans," *American Journal of Psychiatry,* p. 729-733.

Greenson, R. R. (1967). *The Technique and Practice of Psychoanalysis,* Vol. 1. Madison, Conn.: International Universities Press, Inc.

Hamline, R. (1997). *Finding God on a Train: A Journey into Prayer.* San Francisco: Harper.

Herman, J. L. (1942). *Trauma and Recovery.* New York: Basic Books.

Imber-Black, E., Roberts, J., & Whiting, R. (Eds.) (1988). *Rituals in Families and Family Therapy.* New York: W. W. Norton Company, Inc.

Kernberg, O. (1991). Journal of the American Psychoanalytical Association, 39:45-70.

Lifton, R. J. (1964). "On Death and Death Symbolism, The Hiroshima Disaster," *American Psychiatric Journal,* p. 191-210.

Lindemann, E. (1994). "Symptomatology and Management of Acute Grief," *American Psychiatrist,* p. 141-149.

Moreno, L. (1994). *Psychodrama*. Vol.1, Fourth Edition. McLean, Va.: American Society for Group Psychotherapy & Psychodrama.

Padus, E. (Ed.) (1992). *The Complete Guide to Your Emotions and Your Health*. Emmaus, Pa.: Rodale Press.

Pesso, A. (May/1997), Public lecture, *Psychomotor Therapy*.

Pollock, G. H. (1989). *The Mourning-Liberation Process*. Vol. I. Madison, Conn.: International Universities Press, Inc.

——— (1989). *The Mourning-Liberation Process*. Vol. II. Madison, Conn.: International Universities Press, Inc.

Rando, T. A. (1993). *Treatment of Complicated Mourning*. Champaign, Ill.: Research Press.

Russell, P. (1979). *The Brain Book*. New York: Penguin Books.

Schwarts, D. I. (1996). *Finding Joy: A Practical Guide to Happiness*. Woodstock, Vt.: Jewish Lights.

Shapiro, E. R. (1994). *Grief As a Family Process: A Developmental Approach to Clinical Practice*. New York: The Guilford Press.

Suplee, C. (1987). "The Enduring Mystery of Tears," *Washington Post*, April.

Toffler, A. (1970) *Future Shock*. New York: Random House.

United Nations (1982). "The Age of Aging," *U.N. Chronicle*, July.

van der Kolk, B. A. (1987). *Psychological Trauma*. Washington, D.C.: American Psychiatric Press, Inc.

van der Kolk, B. A., McFarlane, A. C. & Weisaeth, L. (Eds.) (1996). *Traumatic Stress: The Effects of Overwhelming Experience on Mind, Body, and Society*. New York: The Guilford Press.

Wycoff, J. (1991). *Mindmapping: Your Personal Guide to Exploring Creativity and Problem-Solving*. New York: Berkley Books.

✦ ABOUT THE AUTHOR ✦

T ian Dayton, who holds a Ph.D. in clinical psychology and an M.A. in educational psychology, is a therapist in private practice in New York City. A fellow of the American Society for Group Psychotherapy and Psychodrama and a faculty member of the Drama Therapy Department at New York University, Dayton presents psychodrama workshops and training nationwide. She is the author of *The Soul's Companion, The Quiet Voice of the Soul, The Drama Within, Keeping Love Alive, Daily Affirmations for Forgiving and Moving On* and *Daily Affirmations for Parents.*

If you would like to be put on a mailing list to receive information about workshops and training, please send your name and address to:

Tian Dayton, Ph.D., T.E.P.
262 Central Park West
Suite 4A
New York, NY 10024

New from the *Chicken Soup for the Soul®* Series

Chicken Soup for the Teenage Soul

Teens welcome *Chicken Soup for the Teenage Soul* like a good friend: one who understands their feelings, is there for them when needed and cheers them up when things are looking down. A wonderful gift for your teenage son, daughter, grandchild, student, friend... #4630—$12.95

Chicken Soup for the Woman's Soul

The #1 *New York Times* bestseller guaranteed to inspire women with wisdom and insights that are uniquely feminine and always from the heart. #4150—$12.95

Chicken Soup for the Christian Soul

Chicken Soup for the Christian Soul is an inspiring reminder that we are never alone or without hope, no matter how challenging or difficult our life may seem. In God we find hope, healing, comfort and love. #5017—$12.95

Chicken Soup for the Soul® Series

Each one of these inspiring *New York Times* bestsellers brings you exceptional stories, tales and verses guaranteed to lift your spirits, soothe your soul and warm your heart! A perfect gift for anyone you love, including yourself!

A 4th Course of Chicken Soup for the Soul, #4592—$12.95
A 3rd Serving of Chicken Soup for the Soul, #3790—$12.95
A 2nd Helping of Chicken Soup for the Soul, #3316—$12.95
Chicken Soup for the Soul, #262X—$12.95

Selected books are also available in hardcover, large print, audiocassette and compact disc.

Available in bookstores everywhere or call **1-800-441-5569** for Visa or MasterCard orders. Prices do not include shipping and handling. Your response code is **HWOUNDS**.

Books to Nurture Your Body & Soul!

Hear the Heartwarming Goodness of Chicken Soup for the Soul® on Audio

Health Communications, Inc. proudly presents its audio collection of the *Chicken Soup for the Soul* series. Each book is available on tape or CD for your convenience. Brighten your life by listening to these words of inspiration.

The Best of the Original Chicken Soup for the Soul® Audio
Code 3723 one 90-minute cassette $9.95
Code 4339 one 70-minute CD $11.95

The Best of A 2nd Helping of Chicken Soup for the Soul® Audio
Code 3766 two 90-minute cassettes....$14.95
Code 4347 one 70-minute CD $11.95

The Best of A 3rd Serving of Chicken Soup for the Soul® Audio
Code 4045 one 90-minute cassette $9.95
Code 4355 one 70-minute CD $11.95

The Best of a 4th Course of Chicken Soup for the Soul® Audio
Code 4711 one 90-minute cassette $9.95
Code 472X one 70-minute CD.............$11.95

Chicken Soup for the Soul® Audio Gift Set
Code 3103 6 cassettes, 7 hours...........$29.95

Available at your favorite bookstore or call 1-800-441-5569 for Visa or MasterCard orders. Prices do not include shipping and handling. Your response code is **HWOUNDS**.